Infinite Desire

Infinite Desire

A Guide to Modern Guilt

Paul Oppenheimer

MADISON BOOKS
Lanham • New York • Oxford

First Madison Books edition 2001

This Madison Books edition of Infinite Desire. A Guide to Modern Guilt, is an unabridged publication of the book originally titled An Intelligent Person's Guide to Modern Guilt and first published by Duckworth in London in 1997, with one textual emendation. It is reprinted by arrangement with the publisher.

Published by Madison Books
4720 Boston Way
Lanham, Maryland 20706

12 Hid's Copse Road
Cumnor Hill, Oxford OX2 9JJ, England
Distributed by National Book Network

Library of Congress Cataloging-in-Publication Data
Oppenheimer, Paul.
  [Intelligent person's guide to modern guilt]
  Infinite Desire : a guide to modern guilt / Paul Oppenheimer.— 1st Madison Books ed.
      p. cm.
  Originally published: An intelligent person's guide to modern guilt. London : Duckworth, 1997.
  Includes bibliographical references and index.
  ISBN 1-56833-173-8 (cloth : alk. paper)
    1. Guilt. I. Title.

BJ1471.5 .O66 2001
128'.4— dc21

00–48609

♾™ The paper used in this publication meets the minimum requirements of American National Standard for Information Sciences— Permanence of Paper for Printed Library Materials, ANSI/NISO Z39.48–1992.
Manufactured in the United States of America.

Contents

Preface

This is a little book of questions and hopes. It makes no attempt at encyclopaedic completeness, and aspects of guilt have doubtless been omitted that may strike some specialists as essential. Apologies are clearly in order for these omissions, and I herewith offer them. As a feeble excuse I can only cite my aim: to provide a guide to the special case of modern guilt, as well as an historical overview of the evolution of guilt generally, and of rebellions against it, and to propose in the last chapter a novel account of the origins of its unusual new forms.

To this must be added what is unexceptionable, that specialisation and broad perspectives each have their proper uses. The quest for meaning cannot be satisfied without both, and the frequent scorn of a few quite rigid specialists for any general picture of a subject only points to their indifference to a basic human need, while their denials that any such perspective can responsibly be established are less persuasive than the yearning for wider comprehension.

To be sure, the test of the broad view, as of the narrow, must lie in its evaluation of evidence, together with its sifting of details, relevant comparisons and teasing out of contrasts. I have thus been led to introduce such information about significant personalities as seems to me pertinent to following the argument and clarifying motives and surrounding social conditions, while rigorously excluding whatever seems extraneous. Jewish and Christian attitudes toward guilt receive more attention than Hindu because Jews and Christians have traditionally concerned themselves with it, while Hindus have not. Goethe's *Faust*, which skirts the issue of Faust's guilt, despite its presentation of murder and infanticide in Part I, likewise reveals less about guilt than do Marlowe's *Doctor Faustus* and Shakespeare's *Hamlet*. Racine's *Phèdre*, which paints a horrifying picture of false guilt, seems less germane to understanding guilt *per se* than Sophocles' *Oedipus the King*, in which the guilt of the hero is genuine and, at least within the play, unquestioned. In these and other instances, including the illustrations from ancient cultures, I have sought to cull evidence according to criteria of influence and worthy insights. Other choices might be made, but any fair account of guilt, it seems to me, can avoid these particular choices only at the risk of misunderstanding the nature of guilt altogether. It is my hope that they may also shed an indirect light on fortuitous omissions.

I am grateful to Robin Baird-Smith, who first suggested that I take on this project; to Deans Martin Tamny and Ilona Anderson, of The City College of New York, who helped to secure a Scholar's Incentive Award that allowed me go ahead with it; to my colleagues in the Department of English at The City College for their support of my award application; to Jennie Weimer for essential research assistance; and to Rose Sawkins, Andras Hamori, Jack Barschi, Katharine Jones, Judy Sproxton, David Curzon and Timothy McFarland (among other helpful colleagues in the Department of German at University College London) for supplying a consistent stream of good ideas, as did my two children, Julie and Ben. Francesca Simpson Pedler read the manuscript, and to her I am grateful indeed for showing me many ways in which to improve it.

London and New York   P.O.
February 1997

I

What is Modern Guilt?

1. The Secular Outlaw

Guilt of any type makes no compromises. The word itself—its original meaning is indebtedness—represents an odd mix of emotions, money, law, and religion. As indebtedness is an absolute condition (either one is in debt or one is not), guilt itself is absolutist, a fact sensed with discomfort by most people, who probably prefer the elasticity of other emotional terms. One may be a little in love or a little bit angry, but from the viewpoint of accuracy the idea of degrees of guilt is meaningless. Any sort of guilt, whether of the emotional, legal, or religious variety, is tensely definite. The word points to a rigidity of indebtedness, and this with an absolutism extraordinary in human affairs.

Guilt's absolutism in fact often seems comparable in power to the storm of an infatuation, though amorous ecstasies probably blow over much faster, and in its legal and physical solidity to birth, death, marriage and pregnancy, which as everyone knows are also absolutist, either clear facts or nonexistent. The ancient Jews and Egyptians believed that guilt resulted from broken pacts with God, the gods or one's ancestors, from human defiance of the supernatural, in other words, as well as from criminal acts. Modern guilt, however, and even in many cases criminal guilt, is a bizarre and new phenomenon. Agnostics, atheists and the religious alike may be caught up in it and not know why. They may only later identify their moments of cold self-mockery with guilt. A secular society, fancying itself impervious to collective guilt, may suddenly find itself deluged by irrational waves of it. Thousands of sensitive, a-religious modern people may seek escape, even through suicide, from a universally spreading guilty energy, whose resemblance to earlier forms of religious guilt seems unaccountable and superficial. They may only know that the world has come to resemble a sterile promontory, in Hamlet's phrase, weary, stale, flat and unprofitable, and that what once looked bearable or wonderful has turned into a sort of morbid shelf crowded with people haunted by self-accusations and unexplained griefs.

In Franz Kafka's story 'The Judgement', teased into life during a single triumphant writing night of 22 September 1912, when, as Kafka later put it, 'the wound burst open', this phenomenon of modern guilt makes one of its earliest, most succinct and dramatic appearances.

On a Sunday morning in spring, a young businessman, Georg, who shares a flat in an anonymous modern city with his father, sits writing a letter to a friend. His mother has recently died, and the friend, who lives far away in Russia, has proved himself a failure at the same type of business—it is never named—at which Georg has proved himself a success. The friend is an isolated, somewhat touchy soul, and this makes it doubly difficult for Georg to tell him both about his own success and his impending marriage. Georg wishes to invite the friend to his wedding, but fears that he may simply provoke him into painful fits of jealousy.

Outside are identical ramshackle houses, a river, a bridge and tender green hills.

Georg finishes his letter, and goes into his father's room to show it to him.

Instantly, we find ourselves, along with Georg, in a den of darkness. His father, a giant of a man, ageing and myopic, sits amidst mementos of his wife, Georg's dead mother, and messy breakfast dishes.

When he rises to greet his son, 'his heavy dressing gown [swings] open as he [walks] and the skirts of it [flutter] round him'. Ignoring his father's leering, suggestive half-nakedness, which imparts a whiff of menace, Georg remarks that 'It's unbearably dark in here', to which the old man responds that 'Yes, it's dark enough.' ' "And you've shut the window too?" "I prefer it like that." '

The reader, but not Georg, who seems lighthearted and abstracted, senses that the father has been waiting, even lurking here 'for months', though the two of them see each other daily 'at business', that he has somehow been expecting him, preparing for some chilly reckoning.

What follows is a brutal conversation at cross purposes, accusatory, confusing, in the midst of which Georg lifts his father, whom he describes as ailing and in need of a doctor, out of his chair, peels off his dressing gown and puts him to bed, pulling off also his father's none-too-clean underwear: 'He carried [him] to bed in his arms. It gave him a dreadful feeling to notice that while he took the last few steps towards the bed the old man on his breast was playing with his watch chain. He could not lay him down on the bed for a moment, so firmly did he hang on to the watch chain.' His father then covers himself with blankets.

The atmosphere throughout, like the room itself, is full of a drab voluptuousness, a morbid sensuality. It reeks of a dour sexiness and sexual repulsion that are crucial to what happens next: an incestuous clash that ends in a dictated suicide.

Remonstrating with Georg for wanting to cover him up, for wishing to hide him away as worthless, his father abruptly throws off his blankets and stands erect on his bed. From this makeshift balcony he berates Georg's fiancée:

> 'Because she lifted up her skirts . . . because she lifted her skirts like this, the nasty creature,' and mimicking her he lifted his shirt so high that one could see the scar on his thigh from his war wound, 'because she lifted her skirts like this and this you made up to her, and in order to make free with her undisturbed *you have disgraced your mother's memory* [italics added], betrayed your friend and stuck your father into bed so that he can't move. But he can move, or can't he?'

These vulgar and ridiculous attacks, loosed along with the cutting accusation that Georg has betrayed his dead mother, turn into a Jobian divine whirlwind of more piercing thrusts:

> 'How long a time you've taken to grow up! Your mother had to die, she couldn't see the happy day, your friend is

going to pieces in Russia, even three years ago he was yellow enough to be thrown away, and as for me, you see what condition I'm in. You have eyes in your head for that!'

Georg responds petulantly at this point—'So you've been lying in wait for me!'—but the reader senses in his shrillness a compromised frailty. At once his father builds to a ferocious crescendo:

'So now you know what else there was in the world besides yourself, till now you've only known about yourself? An innocent child, yes, that you were, truly, but still more truly have you became a devilish human being!—And therefore take note: I sentence you to death by drowning!'

Something frightening and unexpected—but how unexpected is it really?—now occurs:

Georg felt himself urged from the room, the crash with which his father fell on the bed behind him was still in his ears as he fled. On the staircase, which he rushed down as if its steps were an inclined plane, he ran into his charwoman on her way up to do the morning cleaning of the room. 'Jesus!' she cried, and covered her face with her apron, but he was already gone. Out of the front door he rushed, across the roadway, driven towards the water. Already he was grasping at the railings as a starving man clutches food. He swung himself over, like the distinguished gymnast he had once been in his youth, to his parents' pride. With weakening grip he was still holding on when he spied between the railings a motor bus coming which would easily cover the noise of his fall, he called in a low voice: 'Dear parents, I have always loved you, all the same,' and let himself drop.

At this moment an unending stream of traffic was just going over the bridge.

With a desperate and hasty calculation, in other words, and obedient to his father's arbitrary death sentence, its mysterious and steely absolutism, Georg simply kills himself.

It is the ambush of this that is so startling and wrenching, and as rapidly becomes clear, so revelatory in the keenest possible terms of the terrifying predicament of modern guilt itself. It is here that the puzzle begins.

The reason, of course, is the reader's pressing need, and it pulls like an undertow, to make sense of what Georg does. This problem itself quickly becomes compounded and tangled. On the one hand, Kafka's little story seems at first a merely self-indulgent exercise in lunacy, though compelling and credible in ways that seem elusive. On the other hand, the story has usually been frustratingly interpreted in ways that seem both modestly helpful and insufficient. To take the interpretations first: Kafka knew Freud slightly, and as he himself admitted, was influenced by Freudian insights, quite recent at the time of his writing, into suppressed Oedipal conflicts between fathers and sons, and the son's narcissism that could be protracted into later life by its lack of resolution (this view finds support in the father's exclaiming 'How long a time you've taken to grow up!'). More than this, as child and adult Kafka sweated out fierce conflicts with his own father, himself an unpleasant, despotic figure, at least in Kafka's eyes, to whom he addressed his famous undelivered 'Letter to his Father' (completed in 1919 and published posthumously), in which he details these conflicts. The need to write 'The Judgement', therefore, and the sources of Kafka's guilty 'wound' that produced it, can thus be understood, though only, as one guesses, sketchily, if one accepts these explanations of motivation. Right away, however, they begin to feel inadequate, and irrelevant to a much larger issue.

This is that the story has remained intriguing, by way of seeming horrifyingly familiar and baffling with a staggering power, to millions of men who, one may safely assume, have experienced none of these suppressed conflicts, or at least not on the drastic terms offered here, with their fathers, and to millions of women who have likewise not experienced correspondingly guilty struggles with their mothers. These large numbers of readers have probably seen in the story not Kafka's problems with guilt—which would amount to taking it as a fairly narrow case study in psychopathology—but their own. It is these, too, that 'The Judgement', however unconsciously, mirrors and that beg for clarification, and this especially if the mystery and magnitude of the problem of Georg's sham trial in his father's bedroom, along with his guilty conviction and sentencing, are to be grasped in some complete and rational way.

It should be stressed as well that it is guilt, and an evidently singular type of it, that besieges Georg, and not merely embarrassment, remorse or shame. A great many people may confuse embarrassment with guilt, and indeed with any sort of guilt, and possibly commit suicide over some rancid embarrassment. The same must hold true of remorse and shame. These emotions, however, clearly do not embody the more extravagant types of threats that seem to rush so limpidly alive across Kafka's pages. The reason lies in a crucial difference between guilt and any of the deadliest forms of embarrassment, remorse and shame.

The difference is one of concreteness, as it may be termed, and its source is to be found in the fact that all three – embarrassment, remorse and shame – are always embedded in concrete events, and so connected to visible causes. By definition, their scornful but necessarily cramped assaults on the human psyche are thus rather easily traceable. One feels embarrassment over something, and remorse and shame for various types of deeds that one has done, or failed to do, or despised doing, and that others or one's society at large have condemned or would condemn. Guilt of all types, however, while it often includes these dark invasions of the mind that prompt harsh self-laceration, has more bitter and opaque dimensions. It reaches through and beyond merely antisocial behaviour, and so beyond any relatively clearly understood social malfeasance, into supreme violations of ultimate and even universal values. It extends in the broadest sense into rebellious assaults on one's universe and its natural order.

Oedipus, in Sophocles' fifth-century BC Greek tragedy, for example, is judged guilty, albeit according to an ancient code of guilt, and does not not simply suffer embarrassment, or remorse or shame, though he is sensible to each one of them in himself. He unwittingly carries out a prophecy of the gods that he will murder his father and marry his mother – that he will engage in the worst sort of rough taboo-breaking, doing so on a grand scale. Whether conscious of what he is about or not, and with a wicked irony he is not, he proceeds to treat his universe with utter contempt, and to befoul its profoundest, most sacred mystery: its holy capacity to create pure and unstained life. This, as the gods or the universe cannot help but realize, is inherently unforgivable. The result is that his punishments as a guilty violator – his self-inflicted blinding and subsequent doomed exile – are imposed for outrageous corruptions of his universe's most exalted creative impulses. It is these that neither Oedipus' gods nor his universe can tolerate, lest they collaborate in their own humiliation.

How, though, can Georg, or for that matter, his father, be said to face similar problems? In what sense can Georg's grotesque suicide be understood as more than the act of a madman? How is he guilty of anything at all?

To begin to grasp the dilemma that Kafka's ghastly tale exposes so neatly, one needs from the outset to take stock of what it omits: all means of properly identifying both father and son, and of identifying their environment too. We are given no real place names, only the flimsiest data on Georg's early life (he has been a 'distinguished gymnast'), no description of Georg's business, minimal information about his father's past and no information, apart from her death, about Georg's mother. Critics have often argued that these omissions enhance the tale's universality. This can hardly be the case, however, because while the tale depicts a widespread and, as we shall see, increasing phenomenon, that of an hypnotic and possibly new sort of guilt, its murky catastrophe is obviously not ubiquitous. Not so far away, farmers still plough their fields. Mountain climbers and hunters still climb and hunt. Lovers love. Fishermen fish. Happy and unhappy people go on being happy and unhappy. Good novels, films and plays have depicted their lives as well, and their own struggles with traditional forms of guilt – for committing a murder, say, or even for committing treason – and without the tormented battle to the death of Kafka's two self-conscious, grappling souls in this particular story.

The meaning of Kafka's omissions, therefore, must lie elsewhere, possibly in the very fact of their strangeness, in their uncanny spicing of a stew of mordant, vulgar circumstances, and in their sensed contributions to the events of the story themselves.

Their chief contribution is clearly one of a particular type of abstraction that turns out to be guilt-producing. As Georg and his father are described here, they reside in an oddly abstract modern city and live utterly abstract, unvarying lives. Georg's fiancée is an ephemeral unknown. Nature and spring, to be sure, are mentioned briefly, but only, as the reader guesses, with a kind of politeness, to hint at a contrast with the flowering outside world that is unavailable to the main characters.

As a consequence, both Georg and his father seem strangely disembodied and vivid at the same time. They sound like unnamed voices over a telephone, and appear ghostly and unreal, resembling as they do so a very famous group of other people, the work-bound, sighing and guilt-struck crowd that shimmers through T.S. Eliot's *The Waste Land*, published just ten years later, in 1922, with its evocation of modern London:

> Unreal city,
> Under the brown fog of a winter dawn,
> A crowd flowed over London Bridge, so many,
> I had not thought death had undone so many.
> Sighs, short and infrequent, were exhaled,
> And each man fixed his eyes before his feet.

The eyes of Eliot's lost but familiar crowd are fixed before the feet of exhausted, wretched men in another country, in another city, moving over a bridge that spans another river, one that the poet describes cruelly as 'a strong brown god' – and yet the mood of abashed mass worthlessness of these men, their attitude of a guilty mass failure that leads into what the poet describes as their anaesthetized death-in-life condition, with this in a cityscape that is also transformed into an abstraction by the 'brown fog of a winter dawn', feel recognizably close in type to Georg's corrosive inner futility and disgrace, horrible feelings that when stimulated by his father, become unbearable and that dispatch him to his death in his nearby river.

May not these situations be alike in other ways as well?

Certainly they twin with each other in their depictions of a strangely rigid and robotic behaviour. If Eliot's crowd of men that moves over London Bridge appears as a collection of automatons, Georg too turns into a perfunctory doll once he hears his father's death sentence. He feels himself 'urged from the room'. He is 'driven towards the water'. Then he 'let[s] himself drop'. It seems clear that his sense of volition has vanished and that a mental compulsion has taken over. His brain now acts, in other words, only to fulfil a single purpose, that of arranging its own destruction. For this reason he seems, however implausibly, to have lost his mind, or to be insane.

His father has already appeared as somehow irrational, or possibly insane too, particularly as we see him fiddling with Georg's watch chain while Georg hoists him into bed. He grasps at it as if grasping after a fleeting, lethal idea of time itself – desperately and with an idiot's inflated, snarled attention. He seems mad, too, as he accuses his son of besmirching the memory of his mother, the very idea of which is a seeming absurdity, though not without its potentially powerful impact on Georg. In fact, Georg's very existence, as he enters his father's room to show him the letter that he has written, seems to release in the older man a diabolical savagery, turning him into a robot-like creature as well, a soulless marionette rattling off a vicious, automatic judgement, as if the key had been turned in the ignition of an executioner's machine.

It is crucial to understand, though, that if one is serious about regarding Georg's father as insane, one is left with a frustrating quandary, that of being unable to account for Georg's final act, his suicide. This is because while Georg may behave unthinkingly or mechanically in the last few minutes of his life, he is in fact neither suicidal nor irrational. Of this we remain convinced. His demeanour is cool. At several points he even makes trivial if defensive jokes. He seems unimpressed by his father's self-contradictory ramblings, until the gruesome end when his death sentence is pronounced. Only then, as if unable to resist a spurring, vengeful order that he be punished for some fuzzy crime, does he – with a new crisp coolness – rush downstairs to the god-like river and his death.

Unless, in other words, we choose to believe that Georg is himself insane, a possibility for which there is no evidence, we cannot opt for believing in his father's insanity. The logic of the story gets in the way. Even if we move beyond this, and try to dismiss the whole story as an exhibition of lunacy, as a nightmare or morbid fantasy, a purely mental experience, we are kept from doing so, and this time by the incontrovertible horror of Georg's death.

We are also prevented from doing so by a fact even more persuasive, to wit (as we have already noticed) that the emotions of the story feel grotesquely plausible, wickedly familiar, and that its details, even its grimy domestic details, seem to make a silly, awful sense. The upshot of all these paradoxes is that as we try to make sense of events that should make sense, but which resist ordinary efforts in that direction, we find ourselves squeezed between senseless alternatives: either a mad father has elicited a mad response of obedience from a perfectly rational son, which seems preposterous; or a wilful and self-pitying father has been able to persuade his rational, compassionate son that he has been so monstrously neglectful of him that he ought to kill himself, which seems equally unsupportable.

All of this only leads us, appropriately, back to the story itself and its provocative oddity, something that seems as interesting as the omissions. Either Kafka's tale is an artful trap, or it may itself, along with its characters, situation and structure, be a startlingly precise mirror of a certain type of guilt, a hitherto undefined modern guilt, something with which it in fact purports to deal. If, as indeed appears to be the case, this mirror is what Kafka has given us, then we may be able to grasp more clearly the essence of a type of guilt which is intrinsically and perhaps necessarily unclear: a ghostly indebtedness to a hollowed-out, a-religious universe. This new and singular guilt is both spectral and immensely powerful. It puts in only the shadow of an appearance, and yet it sends people to their deaths. It pushes emotional and real suicide on the young as well as the old, and entangles them in snares of silk threads, even those of a dressing gown, that turn out to be as strong as steel. It humiliates millions with the flick of a translucent, skeletal wrist. It arises as a mist of glacial ruthlessness even in the souls of the rational and virtuous, and then moults into a blasting wind. It caresses, beckons and annihilates. Above all, because it is itself disembodied and vague, it stimulates in those who experience it the most mind-sabotaging doubts and dreads.

With these possibilities in hand, we may begin to make sense of the bizarre yet spreading emotion that insists on Georg's death. We may even arrive at an explanation that includes not some but all of the dreadful facts.

What we cannot help noticing is that Georg is a failure who looks like a success. Despite appearances, he has failed to prove himself, both as a man or businessman and as a fully developed, independent human being. Of this at a minimum he is actually guilty. He lacks all heroism, both in his own and his father's eyes, those terrible eyes that look straight through him, challenge him, judge him and finally condemn him. After his apparently protective mother's death and his father's own decline into near helplessness, Georg has promised to take over the family business but has not really done so, an act that would involve rather brusquely pushing his father aside and out. Georg has remained a virtually invisible director of the business, smiling with inward congratulations at the organizational improvements that he has made, but unwilling, indeed unable, to claim public esteem and credit for them. His tolerance, his humanity, make this impossible.

Georg's insurmountable problem in fact is his sheer virtuousness and rationality. He is extremely good. He is neither greedy nor selfish. He has accepted without demur his childhood training at his parents' hands in the estimable if self-weakening concept that love and devotion mean taking endless responsibility for others, first his parents and now his fiancée, and this even to the extent of forever deferring to them in private and everywhere else. He has reduced himself to an abased sketch of a human being, and certainly neglected to let the full human being in himself develop, with his own possibly unique and native ambitions.

His father, on the other hand, perseveres as a demonic power in a godless universe. Nowhere in Kafka's story is any reference made to an outside universe, or to a power greater than his own paternal power. Against the background of a mechanical, nameless, abstract and 'unreal' city, a city that perpetually requires robotic routines for its maintenance, that requires all of its men and women to make themselves over into ceaselessly obedient machines, nature seems a mere trinket, a superfluous decoration. The ageing father's godlike strength, which is a deception because he is not a god, flourishes and seems invincible, especially in the darkened lair of his bedroom, and this only because he has no genuinely divine rivals. Once he is powerfully confronted by the prospect of his own death, and this in a meaningless, anonymous reality set among an unsigned set of urban, artificial and physically decaying forces, and once he becomes aware that all ability to command is draining from him, he lashes out. He assails his once athletically accomplished but now merely civilized son. His son at once agrees, recognizing that his father is right, and also that he cannot change himself. Power, after all, means nothing to him. Greed and selfishness are likewise meaningless and unethical temptations. He has, moreover, no desire simply to humiliate his own father, whom he loves and who by default has become the only power greater than he can ever hope to be in his world. He must humiliate his father, though, if he is to have any real chance of surviving as more than the obedient machine that he has allowed himself to become – if he is himself at last to flourish as an important judge of his own worth, precisely what his father has been.

In this self-defeating situation, Georg's very existence becomes a nullity, a weighty, gross thing. Shocked to his bones to find it openly jeered at, he opts for the one choice that makes a final if horrible sense: his guilt-stained death, the very one that his father assigns to him. This can in fact (for him) be his only solution to his dilemma. Suicide (for him) will provide a perverse, and indeed the only possible, fulfilment.

He at once, therefore, returns to the scene of his childhood swimming successes, the river, and succeeds there again, if perversely, for the last time. Suspended for tormented seconds above this reminiscential river, and then releasing himself into it to drown, he allows his life to yank itself full circle. In contrast to his distant friend, who has at least had the decency to drag his own similar guilty fumbling off to Russia, into an alien society where it can be hidden away as a business failure among strangers who neither know him nor care about him, Georg has dutifully, excruciatingly stayed at home. The ghastliness of this, as we cannot help seeing, is that in a real sense Georg has chosen to flaunt his guilty failure before everyone. His life has amounted to a vulgar if well-intended exhibitionism. To be sure, until his father sentences him to death, he has not completely understood the impact of his behaviour. Once he does, however, he atones for it by ending a degraded existence that for him has entailed the purest possible self-pollution.

Georg's pollution or guilt is obviously unusual, or perfectly modern. In no recognizable sense the guilt either of a traditionally religious or criminal situation, of which there are also a number of modern types, it consists of the severest form of self-betrayal. It seems to arise, take charge of lives and assume the dictatorial powers of a ferocious political tyrant only in the modern urban world in which the absence or death of an abstract one god, together with the industrial and impersonal routines of modern life, renders those who inhabit it themselves abstract and conscience-horrified. For such people, the problem is not the old so-called sins of the flesh but the new, surprising self-corruption of having abandoned their flesh, of having deserted their human vitality as flesh-and-blood creatures. Such people have in fact turned themselves into floating, tormented ghosts. Their self-torture must be daily quashed and suppressed in order to stanch the natural animal pain that accompanies their self-neglect. Their pain, however, and the lethal guilt to which it gives birth, paddle about beneath the surface anyway, with a gritty insistence, and often expressing themselves as bleak, self-directed irony, as self-contempt, or in extreme instances, as abrupt self-destruction.

Nothing could be clearer, too, than that this phenomenon of

modern emotional guilt differs drastically from earlier ones (which may nonetheless coexist with it in modern times in the same person). This new type of guilt, for example, is unlike what Matthew Arnold (1822-88) has in mind when he writes of 'the strength of guilty kings,/When they corrupt the souls of those they rule' (*Merope*), in which guilt is seen in its customary historical role as tempter or seducer. Neither is this new guilt the same as Dryden's 'secret guilt [that] by silence is betrayed' (*The Hind and the Panther*, 1687), with its commonplace bugbear of the guilty secret. Georg's terrible new problem is miles away as well from Thomas Gray's vision of 'Some Cromwell guiltless of his country's blood' (*Elegy Written in a Country Churchyard*, 1751), and its reference to the shedding of innocent blood, and even Sir Walter Scott's phrase 'the guilt of dissimulation' (*The Fortunes of Nigel*, 1822), in which guilt seems to be confused with the more familiar forms of shame, remorse and possibly embarrassment, if it were exposed, and where the use of the word 'guilt' seems to reflect less a desire for emotional diagnosis than, as is often the case, a shrewd writer's desire to produce a strong emotional effect on his readers.

Kafka knew about all this, or so it seems. 'Sometimes,' he wrote, 'I feel I understand the Fall of Man better than anyone.' The theme of his brief writing career in fact is that the Fall never ended. He sets out to examine its latest manifestations in lens-like novels such as *The Trial*, in which the hero, Josef K., is arrested and found guilty without ever knowing why, and stories such as 'In the Penal Colony', with its painful, tattooing machine of eternal punishment, planted far off in a jungle, and its super-vising officer who remarks, 'Guilt is never to be doubted.'

In recent times, Kafka's riveting if melancholy postulate yields the exasperating conclusion that the Fall must indeed be con-tinuing, albeit in fresh guises, and that civilized human beings have grimly managed to push themselves down into unexpected lower depths, or to keep themselves falling. Theirs is not so much a religious or spiritual problem as a psychological and emotional problem in self-extinction. Their human dilemma has worsened. It has also been exacerbated by a well-nigh universal ethical disillusionment.

This is due to the additional fact that the moral relativism of secular, materialistic societies, whether they are democratic or not, has infected vast populations with a rank emotional fever that is the consequence of the abstract lives led by increasing numbers of people, people who are sheltered from life itself and feel themselves isolated in the universe. A scruffy paradox of modern life, at least for educated, secular people, is that their moral relativism has not eliminated guilt but only promoted a new and more vicious version of it. Where the Church and other religions sought (and still seek) to alleviate the old version through confession and atonement, psychiatry sought (and still seeks) to expunge the new one, along with the old, through psychological explanations. This tactic makes for semi-rational semi-science and acrid social confusion. In the modern secular atmosphere of moral anarchy fostered by a basic uncertainty of ethics, of which values to hold dear, the erasure of either type of guilt has not occurred and cannot occur. Where in earlier periods one might have felt guilty for having sinned, one may now easily feel guilty for abandoning all ethical systems, and as a result abandoning oneself. One may feel profoundly guilty for having denied the possibility of guilt.

2. The Religious Terrorist

The slope of the modern soul into a new form of religious guilt begins rather earlier. It parallels the secular, and has a great deal to do with the fact that modern people who believe in God often bicker about his nature. Is God benign or demonic? Was the God of the ancient Jews judgemental or simply just? Is God jealous? Does God have a sense of humour? Does God release us from guilt or insist upon it? Earlier wrestlings over God were generally different in type. They centered on confusing disputes over God's powers, as well as over human problems with belief, doubt and obedience.

It is clearly anachronistic to impute modern squabbles over God to vanished communities that never concerned themselves with them. When Abraham, for example, is told by God to sacrifice his son Isaac, he never wonders whether God's request is insulting, or whether a God who puts him to so sadistic a test is worth his loyalty. Abraham wonders about nothing, it seems, and does as he is told. His willingness to slaughter his son is also not meant to be seen as an isolated instance of stupidity, but as a shining, intelligent example of how to behave when God issues his commands, or so it was apparently understood. The reason is that God was (and for traditional-minded people still is) by definition incomprehensible, as is indicated by his awesome, humiliating appearance at the end of the Book of Job, and that believers could no more discuss his (or her or its) nature than they could speculate meaningfully on obscure divine motives. Despite appearances to the contrary, it is significant that no verse of the Bible directly assigns emotional conflicts to God, and that God is nowhere treated as having a personality or as being human. Even depictions of God as angry or wrathful remain mostly unexplained, and what seems obvious is that no one was asked to accept them as exact duplications of human anger or wrath.

Anthropomorphic treatments of God, or debates over God's nature, are more or less new. This must astonish those who wish to believe that they are only to be found among early peoples, and that modern urban believers are too suave to tolerate divine personifications. Egyptian gods and goddesses are abstract in the sense that the images of them are either distilled approximations of human forms or transfigured renderings of birds and other animals. Jews were always enjoined from depicting God, or making any other graven image, no doubt as a precaution against idolatry. Widespread Jewish art of any sort dates only from the nineteenth century, by which time the legalized move-ment of Jews out of ghettos into the more open secular societies of Europe and America led to a breakdown of this prohibition. While Jewish miniaturists, a number of whom were employed at medieval Christian courts, especially in Spain, painted God and biblical (as well as Arthurian) heroes according to popular Chris-tian traditions, there is no evidence that this was for them anything other than a professional activity.

Medieval Christian depictions of God as an elderly bearded prophet-type were similarly understood among the educated as a shorthand for his incontestable abstraction. Like the medieval mystery plays, in which God also puts in appearances, these paintings were intended to make the divine familiar to illiterate peasants and so to stimulate the dissemination of Christianity. Later Protestant thinkers often misapprehended, and sometimes deliberately misrepresented, the medieval Church's human shorthand for God as indicating an immature stage of belief. If Christianity from its inception also presents God as a person, as Christ, this fact should be understood as having little to do with the idea of personifying God himself. The proof of this is to be found in the impersonal portraits of God throughout the Middle Ages, in which he resembles a formulaic human figure instead of a fully humanized individual, who would have either a pleasant or unpleasant personality, say, and in the portraits of Christ himself, which also display him as a formulaic man, during the Romanesque, Byzantine and Gothic periods, and thereafter as the often controversial fleshly incarnations of the imaginings of hundreds of artists.

The mystery of God, and that of Christ, their inner divorce from personality as well as humanity within their human forms, are not reduced but enhanced by these passionate and vitalizing approaches. Nor are they comparable to recent chummier and icier personifications, according to which God can be dealt with as one might deal with a human friend, comrade or enemy, and complimented as one might a friend or comrade, or joked with and jested about, or even dismissed and killed. Along the same lines, it may be observed that even the ancient pagan cultures of Greece and Rome, with their poet-inspiring, human-like deities such as Zeus and Aphrodite, commonly entertained the notion of an abstract ultimate god. Plato in his *Timaeus* refers to a 'creator', or 'father and maker of all this universe [who] is past finding out'. The carved stone gods of the Aztecs and Mayans reveal a deliberate impersonality or abstraction. While they resemble snakes and in discomforting ways human beings, they remain striking for their differences from actual creatures to be found in the natural world.

The personification of God among Jews and Christians increases in proportion to the decline of religion-based communities and religiously circumscribed human relationships. It corresponds to the decline in the influence of Judaism and Christianity. God becomes more elegantly and vulgarly personal for many Jewish and Christian believers as Western societies turn more 'unreal' and impersonal, and this paradoxically as many of them become more democratic. In 'Dover Beach' (1867), Matthew Arnold mourns this decisive weakening of the magnetism of organized religion, though he was probably not aware of its catalytic power to stimulate a new type of spiritual guilt among the remaining religious:

> The Sea of Faith
> Was once, too, at the full, and round earth's shore
> Lay like the folds of a bright girdle furled.
> But now I only hear
> Its melancholy, long, withdrawing roar,
> Retreating, to the breath
> Of the night wind, down the vast edges drear
> And naked shingles of the world.

Arnold certainly understood that the withdrawal of the Sea of Faith was an anthem of separation, from God and often others. It produced a loss of 'certitude', and this in turn abetted fearsome, novel forms of individual sequestration, in which 'we are here as on a darkling plain/Swept with confused alarms of struggle and flight/Where ignorant armies clash by night'. Arnold also understood that titanic new forces of evil had now been loosed. He may not have thoroughly understood that these would promote their own personifications, or that Satan was suddenly as likely to be personified, or to assume a human form, as God.

It is apparently the case, though, that the personification of Satan, like that of God, is also rather recent. The medieval Satan of Dante's *Inferno*, for instance, scarcely resembles a human being. He stands enormous, leaching and frozen in the swamp of Cocytus at the bottom of Hell. He presents three ghastly faces and six eternally beating, bat-like wings. With his three mouths he simply masticates, devouring forever the bodies of the arch-traitors of the ancient world, Judas, Brutus and Cassius. Even

Milton's Satan in *Paradise Lost*, though often sentimentalized as a revolutionary because of his uninteresting declaration that it is 'better to reign in Hell than serve in Heaven', looms amid hellish tortures as a serpentine creature of repulsive ugliness. It is evident that the Satanic guilt born of a treacherous rejection of God in these cases is traditional. It consists in the sort of bellicose pride, or hubris, that leads straight into the lunatic belief that one may actually replace God, and so eliminate a natural divine order.

With Feodor Dostoyevski (1821-81) a terrible, resonant change is rung in. Several of Dostoyevski's protagonists, or anti-heroes, among them Raskolnikov in *Crime and Punishment* (1866) and the tempter Ivan in *The Brothers Karamazov* (1880), actually confuse themselves with Satan, or at least with evil incarnate, and suffer excruciating conflicts over their wilful and enjoyable spasms of super-selfconscious guilt. The idea of their behaviour may easily seem artificial, but it should be noted that nothing is odder in any event than the theatrical, stagy world of Dostoyevski's fiction – unless, as his art succeeds in establishing, it is the modern world itself.

Everything in Dostoyevski's novels has a modern contrived air. Emotions, whatever they may be, develop amid elephantine strains. No emotion is ever pleasing in itself. It must immediately be rejected and replaced by its opposite, which is also rejected and replaced by yet a third, and with this fished out of the blue or extracted magically from a sleeve. In the end, the reader understands, it makes no difference what these emotions are, as long as they remain extreme. Love, hate, anger, jealousy, envy, lust – all must flit past in a kaleidoscopic intense instant. Longing collapses into disgust. Adoration droops into mouldy distaste. Stability is despised as hypocrisy. Even rebellion and social revolution are seen as paltry delusions of escape from a new reality that is disastrous and disastrously empty.

Quite possibly the most diabolical of Dostoyevski's characters from this point of view is Nicolai Stavrogin in *The Possessed* (1871-72). He may also be the most revealing of the new phenomenon of modern religious guilt. If nothing else, Stavrogin illustrates the truth of the German poet Heinrich Heine's ironic observation that 'God cannot be saved by the devil'.

In the fateful sixth chapter, which most lucidly exposes the modern religious guilt-problem, Stavrogin unburdens himself of his torments. He confesses to a crime of ravishing terror, or almost confesses: he withholds one page of the confession that he asks a retired bishop, Tihon, to read.

We are scarcely surprised. Stavrogin has spent the previous night in a state of rigid anxiety, 'often staring hard at one point in the corner by the chest of drawers'. When he arrives at the gates of the local Spas-Yefimyev Bogorodsky Monastery, where Tihon is staying, he becomes alarmed, thinking that he may have left his written confession in his room, then grins with baffling relief as he discovers it in a side-pocket. His mood seems a riddle to the reader. So does Tihon. His two-room apartment appears less the haunt of a man of God than a pavilion of earthly delights.

This matters because it suggests his own earthiness. As we shortly realize, evil to him is no abstraction but a dread against which he must arm his soul, even to the extent of subjecting it to temptation. To him, naïveté, like cynicism, is perilous. A modest man, but not weak, he wanders among fine inlaid tables, costly bibelots, engravings, rare silver and gold icons and a worldly collection of books, including novels and reportedly items 'much worse'. His two rooms are a type of spiritual laboratory, we come to see, and Tihon himself a new sort of spiritual chemist, who is curious and wary, yet eager to keep up with what is lately most threatening to the spiritual integrity of human beings.

After some startled hesitations, Stavrogin produces his confession. It is very long, and full of irrelevant-seeming ramblings. Tihon's reading of it consumes most of the chapter, which is therefore presented from Stavrogin's own warped line of insight. This fact is important, though the reader hardly grasps it at first, because Stavrogin's confession is really a seduction, a voluptuous invitation to guilt and horrible glee. It amounts to fresh excuse-making for evil, and is monstrous, cunning, febrile and barbaric, yet couched in the sympathetic and self-deprecatory terms of nervous bathos.

In the midst of it all shivers the ghost of a dead child, a

twelve-year-old girl whom he has enticed into a catastrophic sexual freedom, and then abandoned to her own guilt and suicide. Again, we do not understand until later that his calculated seduction of this girl is born of a demonic, new, spiritual guilt, or that it has emerged, like some deathless harpy that feeds forever on his demented ethics, from his own corrupt sense of worthlessness. It is the latter that is peculiarly modern too, both as a fashion in belief and, unsettling as this may seem, frightening as it must become, as a threat to civilization. Stavrogin is not one of civilization's discontents, to use Freud's term for those whose repression of instincts leads them into neurosis. He is one of civilization's potential destroyers. He worries a bit about his own sanity, yet is clearly rational and ethically sensitive, and this is mildly reassuring. Nonetheless, for the past year he has been suffering from the hallucination of an 'evil being' that 'shows different faces and yet is always the same and always infuriates me. ... It's myself in various forms. ... I do believe in the devil. I believe canonically, in a personal devil, not in an allegory, and I don't need confirmation from anybody.' He is tormented by this devil hallucination. Even his confession, we are assured by the *persona* of the author of the novel itself, is 'a morbid thing, the work of the devil who had taken possession of this gentleman. ... The fundamental idea of the document is a terrible undisguised need of punishment, the need of the cross, of public chastisement.' At the same time, and this too, like Stavrogin's mood, is a riddle, he may not really 'believe in the cross', may not believe in God and may no longer consider himself a Christian.

His confession, which has been printed in secret but which is meant for an eventual public release, describes his dissipated life as a retired army officer in the 1860s in St Petersburg. It starts off with a petty act of betrayal. His landlady's daughter, the twelve-year-old Matryosha, is wrongly accused by her mother of having stolen his penknife. She whips her daughter unmercifully. When Stavrogin subsequently finds the knife, he makes no attempt to exonerate Matryosha, but instead throws it away. His feeling as he does so is rather unnerving: 'I experienced a pleasurable sensation because suddenly a certain desire pierced me like a blade, and I began to busy myself with it.'

He busies himself oddly, by allowing 'base' emotions to take possession of him, by letting them gather into a 'frenzy' which he has no wish to control, and by rejoicing in Matryosha's shame at having been punished by her mother in his presence. Simultaneously, he is bored: he vacillates emotionally. He studies theology, but this only increases his nipping *ennui*. Then he returns to Matryosha's house (it contains one of the three flats he is renting), and finds her alone:

> I quietly sat down on the floor beside her. She started, and at first was incredibly frightened and jumped to her feet. I took her hand and kissed it, drew her down to the stool again, and began looking into her eyes. The fact that I kissed her hand suddenly made her laugh like a baby. But her amusement lasted only an instant: she quickly jumped up again and this time in such a fright that her face was convulsed. She stared at me, her eyes motionless with terror, and her lips began to twitch as though she was going to cry, but she did not. I kissed her hand again and seated her on my knees. She suddenly pulled away from me with a jerk of her whole body and smiled as though ashamed, but it was a strangely wry smile: her whole face reddened with shame. I was whispering to her and laughing. Suddenly something happened that astonished me – a thing so odd that I shall never forget it: the little girl threw her arms around my neck and suddenly began to kiss me violently of her own accord. Her face expressed perfect rapture. I got up, almost indignant – this behaviour in so young a creature repelled me, the more so because my repulsion was born of the pity which I suddenly felt …

Here Stavrogin's confession is interrupted because he has left out a page. This would seem to be a crucial omission, but he assures Tihon that 'nothing happened. Nothing.' 'Well, God be praised,' says Tihon, crossing himself, but he has previously remarked that the missing sheet does not matter because 'it's all the same now'.

Indeed it is, in the sense that the toxic damage has already been done. Stavrogin has raped Matryosha's delicate spirit, if not her body. Her spirit has yearned only to adore him, and looked to be admired by him. In discovering her own erstwhile unknown appetites for shame and her own enjoyable guilt, Matryosha has awakened impulses in herself that convince her that she, like Stavrogin, may be unworthy of God, and may even be an enemy of God. Her purity has been spoiled in her own eyes. As a result, when Stavrogin next encounters her, she reacts with fright and rage, and shakes her fist at him in silence. Stavrogin himself at this point seems both to care about her and to hate her. Often, he confesses, he becomes so frightened of what has happened between them that 'I decided to kill her. At dawn I ran with that purpose to Gorokhavaya Street. On my way I kept imagining myself in the act of killing and defiling her. My hatred rose especially at the memory of her smile: my contempt mixed with measureless disgust as I remembered the way she had thrown herself on my neck with heaven knows what notion.' His own fear – and he observes that it mixes with a delicious tremor of guilt as well – overcomes him, and he at once becomes ill. His desire to kill her now abates. Then, he learns, Matryosha has become ill herself. When he visits her, her mother tells him that 'her ravings were horrible; she kept saying: "I killed God" '. It is only a few days later that he hears that she has hanged herself.

The rest of his confession is a lurid mishmash of his tusslings and bickerings with the guilt that now unquestionably batters him about, and that the reader cannot help seeing as part of his larger enigma: his religious contradictions. He lunges in one direction with this guilt, then another. On the one hand, he strives to legitimize himself in a traditional, religious way. When he discovers that he is under no suspicion by the police for having caused Matryoscha's death, he surrenders to episodes of anger, venting his spluttering spleen on anybody whom he meets. Shortly afterwards, he gets married. He chooses Marya Timofeyena Lebyadkin, another of his landladies (not Matryosha's mother). She is lame, a 'rapturous idiot' and the 'lowest of the low'. He sees himself, grandiosely, as her saviour. With self-nauseating theatricality, he regards his wife as his punishment. This act of marriage only leads him, on the other hand, to turn himself into an outlaw – and so to scandalize himself – by deserting his wife directly after their wedding. He goes abroad, and wanders from country to country for years. The sacrificial image of Matryoscha begins to haunt him. It invades even his most blissful, escapist dreams, and the little girl suddenly appears in them 'haggard and with feverish eyes, precisely as she had looked at the moment when she stood on the threshold of my room, and shaking her head, had lifted her tiny fist against me. The pitiful despair of a helpless creature with an immature mind, who threatened me (with what? what could she do to me, O God?), but who, of course, blamed herself alone!'

Unable to rid his mind of these visions, and also not wishing to rid his mind of them or their curiously soothing guilt, Stavrogin debates with himself whether to commit a new crime, this time that of bigamy, but at the last minute decides against doing so. He hesitates over his future, but eventually returns to Russia. There, as if seeing himself clearly for the first time, he writes out his confession and has it printed, and waits – but for what? Why, in the end, has he come to Tihon with his peculiar document? What, apart from some pointless desire for useless punishment, lies at the bottom of it, or of his guilt?

Tihon is plainly aghast at the confession and Stavrogin himself. He remarks that Stavrogin is one of those who are 'ashamed of repentance'. This is no doubt true: Stavrogin has perhaps always considered himself worthless, indeed far too worthless, so worthless that he is no longer able to accept the redemption of his own religion. The compassion of the Christian or any other god will for him forever prove inadequate.

What also seems clear, however, and this fact becomes crucial, is that nothing of what Stavrogin has done can be understood apart from the decayed neighbourhood that he has previously chosen as the site for his crime against Matryosha and in which he now again has chosen to live. This ex-army officer, who is also a 'gentleman', has in fact been slumming. He has been amusing himself among the helpless. He has deliberately vanished into squalor. He has cut himself off from his own class, and from his original mission in life, which was paradoxically to revive the Christian spirit in Russia. He has hidden himself away in a run-down section of St Petersburg, among the depraved and poor, and there invented a revolting new mission for himself, at precisely the moment when he spotted in the mirror of the rotted streets, the flayed houses and ruptured humanity the rotting darker underbelly of his own brutalized nature. There is, moreover, no question of his nature's being brutalized rather than naturally brutal: Stavrogin is an educated man, a compassionate man, with a highly developed aesthetic sense. His spelling may have grown weak by now, and his grammar flickery, but at some stage of his life he read books bound in gilt morocco and absorbed the noble, soul-stirring sentiments in them.

What is illuminating about this neighbourhood, his chosen arena of human misery, as in Kafka's 'The Judgement', is what is missing from it: some hint of the divine. It is not there. No sacred candles glow against this rheumy dark. No hymns are sung by anyone. No one prays or yearns for a higher level – other than a purely materialistic level – of existence. All is flat, dreary, crowded and shabby. Life is tasteless and sickly. The place, if not the world itself, verges on inarticulate violence. Nature, as with Kafka's truncated reality, is also missing. In Dostoyevski, it should be added, there is generally a lack of interest in nature. Flowers, hedgehogs, foxes and even dogs announce themselves but seldom in his novels. In *The Possessed*, however, this deliberate neglect assumes a morbid significance. It becomes a negative, powerful symbol of a modern urban amputation of the universe itself from ordinary, and especially poverty-stricken, lives. Confronted with this environment too, even Tihon has felt helpless (and hence perhaps his retirement). At most he can occasionally try to nudge a few people toward God, doing so with a casual remark or two. He cannot, however, exhort them in some traditional way. They would not understand. Everyone whom he knows lives amid a filthy darkness of things, piffling life away amid a sense of abandonment.

Tihon can, however, express alarm. He has carefully cultivated an old sense of the divine-uncanny in himself, where Stavrogin has nourished his own modern sense of the satanic-uncanny. As Tihon reads Stavrogin's hectic account of his treachery and watches him, his mystical intuition leads him to sound a tocsin. 'Christ too,' he says, 'will forgive you if you will reach the point where you can forgive yourself,' but almost at once he finds himself adding in grief and horror: 'I see ... I see clearly ... that never, poor lost youth, have you stood nearer to a new and more terrible crime than at this moment.'

Stavrogin immediately rages at him as a 'cursed psychologist'. He storms out of Tihon's apartment (and so the chapter ends) – but what can Tihon mean? What has he seen or understood?

Slyly, humbly, among his bibelots and icons, he has glimpsed Stavrogin's terrible new hedonism. This is not the hedonism of mere self-indulgence and the self-indulged senses, which may mar no one's peace, and may even reinforce it, but that of Stavrogin's modern devil, which, like the old one but in a thoroughly modern way, seeks to set the heavens on fire. The elderly bishop has glimpsed in Stavrogin the guilty pleasure of modern heavenly defiance, which plays itself out as ferocious disloyalty to others, as contempt for society and the human world, and which is indulged in solely for the sake of guilt itself. Virtue in Stavrogin's eyes has deteriorated into a mockery, redemption into a vanished and ridiculous holy grail. The spiritually elect, who might have won the grail in the past, have long since disappeared. Their knightly age of devotion has withdrawn, like Arnold's Sea of Faith, and has actually vaporized. As a result, the earth has fallen into a new and peculiarly vacant wretchedness. Guilt is the only condition that can be trusted in these circumstances, or that Stavrogin can trust, and he feeds his sense of it through acts of murderous humiliation, with all of their miasmal consequences, so that it may indeed become a threat to civilization. In fact, the idea of an entirely humiliated society based on guilt appeals to him. Such a world will resemble a type of spreading spiritual slum, to match the physical slum in which he resides. Conscience in Stavrogin's modern mental abattoir has become sheer obedience to the necessities of the humiliation of others and of his own self-punishment.

Behind his fantasy of desecration, though, lies his belief in metastasizing, painful separations. His inevitable separation from others matches up with his guilty separation from God. His modern religious guilt, or by extension anyone else's, originates in the feeling that he is thoroughly abased before others, and hence before God, because he is doomed to betray both anyway, and in his feeling that no amount of philanthropy – or good deeds, or acts of repentance – can overcome these inevitable separations. Religion may enchant others with its prayers and ceremonies, but for him it can no longer light the way. In the modern world of pure materialism, it has become an unreliable guide, which is not the same defect as, in the past, its often being either a banality or a corrupt manipulator of political states and naïve worshippers. Religion can never, as also in the past, span the terrible gap, an ever-widening one, in many cases growing so wide as to become a violent schism, an eruptive wound, between himself and others and between himself and God. His problem is thus neither psychological nor social, but as Paul Tournier points out (in *A Doctor's Casebook in the Light of the Bible*), purely spiritual. A refined consciousness of the modern human being as a self has led to a demolishing of all the ancient bonds. Only a transcendental mystical experience, and this only rarely, might overcome it, and this only for seconds or at most moments (Dostoyevski himself, it should be noted, was a Christian mystic). For Stavrogin, the universe has been disconnected from us even as we have come to understand it better from a scientific point of view.

There is another way for him, though, apart from religion, to bridge the gap: that of crime. In the end, this is what Stavrogin, however horribly, has come to believe. It has become his new mission. A series of crimes, or of bestial and unending acts of social rapacity, may create perverse but solid new connections, between himself and others, and between himself and the divine. His path, and that of the modern and wretchedly religious, is the path of the criminal. It is in this sense, Tihon realizes, that Stavrogin's confession is a seduction, or a brazen attempt to convert others, including him, to a life of religious treason. Tihon is of course aware of what Stavrogin is up to, and, as might be imagined, is far less intrigued than sickened. He sees through Stavrogin's logic to its crusty meaning. He understands too that however destructive Stavrogin's plan may be, however productive of guilt simply for its own sake, Stavrogin has committed himself utterly to it. He has committed himself to the ruin of humanity. If he succeeds, the outcome can only be a new barbarism.

What neither man can apparently foresee is that this new barbarism, if it becomes fashionable, may easily combine with its complement: with new types of laws. Stavrogin's promotion of an unending stream of guilty acts may develop its own legitimacy. It may even come to seem normal to vast numbers of people. It may be applauded as a better condition of social health. Over the past couple of centuries, it may be argued (for this problem begins to develop long before Dostoyevski writes *The Possessed*), this has indeed occurred. It is Kafka's chief modern perception. It is expressed, with dismay and eloquence, in *The Trial*. Stavrogin's posing of the question of modern religious guilt, therefore, and not only his criminal's brash answer to it, meshes inevitably with questions of modern criminal guilt itself, and with questions about the odd nature of many modern laws. These questions, like Stavrogin's grotesque new mission, arise from a marked and widespread new enthusiasm for guilt as well as for social justice: from an adoration of guilt for the ghostly new tyranny that it may produce.

3. Modern Laws and the Love of Guilt

Aside from lawyers, most people if asked would probably confess themselves out of sympathy with laws, and even with the idea of laws. This would not mean that they would see no necessity in them, only that laws of any sort evoke prickly sensations among those who imagine, in most instances quite properly, that laws are meant for criminals, and that as they are not criminals, there is no need to surround their own lives with all manner of irrelevant bluster.

A worse reaction would probably ensue if the same people were asked about the presumed relations between laws and ethics. In all likelihood, they would see none. They might cheerlessly concede that a constant clamour – audible mostly from politicians and lawyers (and in democratic countries the one is often the other) – arises in the newspapers, on the internet and on television that the reverse is the case, that laws are merely the expression of ancient ethical codes. They might agree that laws against murder imitate the Commandment that says, 'Thou shalt not kill.' At the same time, they would probably, and rightly, see no connection between ethics of any sort and laws regulating drinking, singing, smoking, fishing, dressing, kissing and flirting (as at American universities and in some towns, where flirting is now banned as 'sexual harassment').

Ethics, they would probably maintain, have given way to whimsies, trends, fads, power-seeking and politics. To some extent, and in a few societies to a great extent, this was always true. Laws, and the guilt as well as innocence that they imply, were always avenues of opportunism. In the past two centuries, however, or more specifically since the enactment of the Code Napoléon in France, with its broad influence, and the Civil Code in Germany, which was widely imitated elsewhere as well, the legal and as a result the social atmosphere of many countries, and of all economically advanced countries, has altered drastically. On a personal level, this has been one result of a vastly greater number of official routines imposed on most middle-class people, together with the new laws and punishments that they entail.

For the middle-class millions, in fact, the old transition from the natural routines of childhood – from eating, sleeping, day-dreaming, playing, chatting with parents and making fun of grumpy aunts and uncles – to the increasingly regimented schedules and other requirements of schools, universities and jobs (now termed careers to allow underpaid job-holders to feel a fleeting sense of importance) seems no longer an invitation to self-fulfilment but an abandonment of it. One's apprehension of guilty self-desertion may not begin here, but it certainly receives a brisk boost. So, of course, does the desire to rebel, though relatively few have the courage to express it in view of the punishments quickly administered. The sheer number of punishments, in fact, many of them for behaviour that was not understood as criminal in the past, has also increased. With it, a pervasive sense of social guilt has unquestionably infiltrated modern societies, a bit like a precocious mist or ghost, but one that stalks by day, and incessantly, as well as by night. The accruing constriction of liberties in the modern political state, in any state at all, whether it is democratic or not, is one of its most obvious characteristics.

To see this change more clearly, one need only think of what one cannot legally do now that one might have done with impunity a couple of centuries or even a few years ago. A short-list of these new crimes may serve to delineate the many new dimensions of modern legal guilt itself, and the novel guilty atmosphere that is its latest result. This list, to be sure, must amount to a jumble of horrors along with well-established social habits, but all of them only recently prohibited (many of them appropriately so): littering, slogging across the grass of certain public parks, money-laundering, serving drinks to the inebriated, watering one's lawn whenever one likes, unlicensed peddling, genocide, unlicensed fishing and hunting, swimming where one pleases, gassing enemy troops to death in war, spitting, wenching, shouting, whaling, unrestricted smoking, child labour, firing workers without notice, murdering one's wife's lover (until recently legal in Brazil), hiking across privately owned land, conspiracy (of many types), contributory negligence (as when one starts a forest fire by throwing away a lit match), forming monopolies in business, price fixing, libel and slander (both far more tightly restricted in recent decades), keeping odd animals as pets (such as tigers, giraffes and crocodiles), selling certain sorts of pornography (however pornography is defined), drinking alcohol at any age, travelling without a passport, killing wolves, unrestricted gambling and betting, unrestricted parking of cars, racial and other types of discrimination, allowing noxious fumes to pour from fireplaces and factories, unrestricted gun ownership, deserting one's husband and children, selling rotten food, overloading ferries and ocean liners, consuming and selling narcotic drugs, marrying at any age, operating unlicensed motor vehicles, driving unsafe but romantically appealing vehicles, dumping oil and sewage into oceans and rivers, committing suicide, pandering, spanking children (a serious crime in several countries), operating unlicensed radio and television stations, murdering praying mantises, refusing to wear seat belts in cars and importing exotic plants.

A good many of the laws describing these crimes are not enforced, or only selectively enforced. People are still getting away with murder, in other words, as they always have and always will. Yet that is scarcely the point, which must be that this is a short-list. Thousands more laws that specify new crimes exist as well, possibly tens of thousands. In many cases the concept of the crime with which these laws deal did not exist until the twentieth century.

Omitted from this list, too, are other new and often justifiable categories of laws and crimes: medical malpractice (largely limited to the US, but setting a rapid pace in other countries), wiretapping (not by the government), industrial espionage and a host of laws regarding computer invasions and computer privacy. There are many other omissions: the European Union regulates working hours; the German government controls shop-closing times. Indeed, fresh criminal descriptions pour forth from parliaments and legislatures across the world in an annual avalanche. It may be suggested that few lives are untouched, few minds unimpinged by this development, which is itself new, and that the guilt-mist palpable to everyone is constantly thickening.

In America since the 1970s, this new legislative avalanche has been accompanied by a blizzard of new litigation. Of course, Americans have always been litigious. Suing people and governments is part of their tradition of democracy, though it is frequently incomprehensible to Europeans. Lately, however, it has become incomprehensible to Americans themselves. Inundated with mounting waves of appeals, the American Supreme Court has set limits to the number of cases per term that it is willing to hear. Medical malpractice cases, many of them frivolous (many of them not), clog the lower courts. Class-action law suits, representing millions of people, consume vast amounts of legal energy on behalf of customers accusing pharmaceutical and other companies of cheating them with deceptive advertising and defective products. School districts have been sued for failing to educate. The police have been sued for brutality. Limits have been set, as in England, on the amounts of money permissible as

awards in cases of wrongful damage inflicted on arms, legs,
nerves, toes and fingers. The spectacle of entire societies spend-
ing all of their waking hours bustling, seething, groaning,
harrumphing and carping their way through the law courts is by
no means any longer outlandish.

Excellent justifications can be offered for these activities. The
chief justification, quite naturally, is the righting of perceived
social and economic inequities. Little attention is paid to the
costs in personal harassment, or to the creation of a new atmosphere of impending, generalized guilt. In his essay 'Civil
Disobedience' (1849), Thoreau anticipated some such ransacking
of individual freedoms when he asked, 'Must the citizen ever for
a moment, or in the least degree, resign his conscience to the
legislator? Why has every man a conscience, then?' Thoreau's
questions are airily dismissed by masses of laws whose intentions may be good, but whose cumulative effects are personal
inhibitions and numbness. Every product in one's home, for
instance, from its tables and chairs to its toothpaste, smoke
detectors and mattresses, has become the repository of an invisible cache of guilt-provoking laws. One inhabits less a home than
an unacknowledged courtroom, supervised by gangs of ghostly
legislators, prosecutors and judges. The castle of privacy has long
since dissolved into a law-bound hive of guilt-interested bureau-
crats, who perch unseen on the sofas and hide in the refrigerator.

The Italian jurist Bruno Leoni points out (in *Freedom and the
Law*) that the modern obsession with legislating criminality, as
opposed to a traditional approach in which it was far more often
determined by judges who had no legislative powers, accelerated
following World War II. Totalitarian majorities became more
fashionable than totalitarian governments. The very word 'law'
changed its meaning, together with its purpose.

To such an extent was this true that modern lawyers and the
public are scarcely any longer aware of the earlier ideas of these
things, or that they demonstrated greater flexibility in treating
legal problems and were far less intrusive into the private lives
of citizens. In the not-so-distant past, law was not so readily
identified with legislation, while 'legislation appears today to be
a quick, rational, and far-reaching remedy against every kind of

evil or inconvenience, as compared with, say, judicial decisions, the settlement of disputes by private arbiters, conventions, customs, and similar kinds of spontaneous adjustments on the part of individuals'. Often ignorant but prejudiced majorities in legislatures thus promulgate new legislation, and hence new possibilities of criminal guilt, at every juncture. The popular new notion of legislation, indeed, is that it may serve as a panacea, muffling the complaints of some temporarily influential group or other, even if it must shortly be amended or repealed because the group in question has dissipated its attractions.

The ancient Romans, and later the English, and until recently the Americans, instead took the view that law, which was not legislation, ought properly to be discovered rather than enacted, and that the act of discovery could most wisely be handled by trained judges whose powers over their societies as a whole were limited. The widespread influence in the past of Justinian's *Corpus Juris* across Europe, which complemented this English and American practice, led to the formerly well established concept of 'lawyer's law', or *Juristenrecht* in Europe, according to which lawyers devoted their careers to these legal 'discoveries'. It persisted even through the period of the divine right of kings, from the sixteenth to the eighteenth century. By contrast, modern legislation almost everywhere has become a type of absolutist *diktat*, imposed by the majority on the rest of a population. The excuse put forward, in addition to that of righting social and economic wrongs, that modern technological societies require new, more far-reaching and more complex laws – that the old approach must now be regarded as obsolete – is in truth nothing but a rationalization of the seizure of increasingly sprawling, guilt-producing powers by legislatures and parliaments. The fact remains that original scientific, technological and artistic work is usually the product of small, and often initially unpopular, groups of people. Novel, imaginative pursuits are unlikely to benefit, or even to occur, if individual judgement is more and more hedged about with new pieces of legislation.

Far worse is the likelihood of popular distaste with this new legal situation itself. It must lead to spreading demoralization.

This is because any society changes. Continuous and inevitable social change in an environment of continuously multiplying laws means a continuously heightened sense of social constriction, then of alienation and then of potential guilt. This dismal process must in turn breed a continuously burgeoning disrespect for government and laws themselves. It will come as no real surprise that the values of the population must now slowly change. At first, a virus of cynicism must spread and itself infect both trust and confidence. Next, an esteem of outlawry must gradually and then more quickly take hold. What is important as all this happens is that none of it will have anything necessarily to do with economics. A prosperous country may as easily fall victim to the sense of profound frustration and consequent malaise. The sole issue must be the unchecked expansion of rules, laws and possibilities of guilt. Those who face condemnation no matter where they turn will show no hesitation in flaunting their final, unalienable freedom, which is disobedience.

An interesting precedent for this type of rebellion induced by a sense of inescapable guilt exists in the area of relgion. Researchers such as Anthony Masters (in *The Natural History of the Vampire*) point out that during the fifteenth century many thousands of people committed themselves to witchcraft and satanism because the Church, which had previously paid little attention to these gloomy activities, suddenly declared war on them, and because as a result many people became convinced that the road to salvation was too steep and pocked with clerical rules and regulations, whose exacting demands they could never hope to meet. Witchcraft and satanism provided at least the possibility of a pleasure-giving alternative of defiance for those who simply assumed their own guilt and damnation.

In recent decades, prison literature has enjoyed a popular and similar notoriety. The memoirs of Jean Genet (*Our Lady of the Flowers*), for instance, were published in 1943, but gained a wide readership only after the end of the War. Genet actually celebrates the idea of criminality, as do large numbers of recent, popular films (such as *Bonnie and Clyde*, 1967). These works of art seem symptomatic of a peculiarly modern disaffection with laws *per se* and with their implications of a univerally smothering atmosphere of legal guilt.

Criminals, to be sure, whether convicted or not, have always romanticized their crimes, often to excuse them, on occasion to glory in them. In recent years, however, the flavour of this outlaw delectation has altered. The public has joined in the criminal's festivities, bizarrely admiring criminality for its own sake. Where the Robin Hood of legend was applauded for robbing the rich to give to the poor, modern thieves, kidnappers and murderers are often admired simply for thumbing their noses at the law. Their guilt seems a badge of social freedom. It is viewed not so much as a debt to be paid as a certificate of anti-social heroism. Often it masquerades as an arbiter of social change, when its real aim is the promotion of social collapse. The cultivation of criminal guilt has thus become a frequently approved form of social rebellion among those disllusioned with all ideologies and all forms of social organization. Society itself, with its guilt-producing laws, any society, is the enemy, and getting away from human institutions, or destroying them, the only goal. A paradisal freedom from restraints and obligations remains the dream beyond the goal, to be realized by whatever means necessary.

How sweet, by contrast, if also threatened with horror, are the few minutes of genuine, guilt-free bliss enjoyed by the two fishermen in Guy de Maupassant's short story 'Two Friends'. Set during the Franco-Prussian War (1870-72), the story paints an idyllic though brief release from laws and guilt into a type of human freedom that is fast becoming an unfamiliar relic from a lost age, and that even in Maupassant's own day was rapidly and tragically disappearing. His story may thus serve as a standard against which to measure the subsequent modern decline into a condition in which an ever-wriggling sense of guilt, and a steady guilt haze, have come to be accepted as usual, as invisible yet powerful ingredients of most lives. Relatively few modern people can have experienced the freedom depicted by Maupassant, and most of the rest probably do not even realize that they have not experienced it.

The two friends of the story run into each other in Paris on a Sunday morning. They are fishing friends who have not seen

each other for quite a while. One, Morissot, is a watchmaker left
unemployed by the war, the other, Sauvage, a haberdasher.
Before the Prussians advanced to just outside the city with their
siege guns, before 'the mess we're in', as Sauvage puts it, both
had spent every Sunday, through spring, summer and autumn,
'till the setting sun reddened the sky and stained the river
crimson', after taking a short train-ride out of town, at Marante
Island, fishing indolently and enjoying the beauty of the scene
and their own Sunday idleness.

Now, on the spur of the moment, and also because the weather
is perfect, they decide to go fishing again: an unthinkable idea
since it will mean straying over the French lines of battle.
Sauvage is undeterred. 'The French outposts aren't far from
Columbes,' he says. 'I know Colonel Dumoulin: they'll let us
through without any trouble.'

Dumoulin is happy to let them through with their angling
gear, and they at once, in dread of being fired upon by the
Prussian enemy, find themselves dodging and running toward
the river bank across the level ground of a vast and broodingly
fallow plain that stretches as far as Nanterre. Neither man has
ever seen any Prussians, but they know that their guns and
forward units are stationed above them in the hills. Marante
Island, when they reach it, is completely deserted, as is a little
restaurant nearby.

The two men spend a marvellous, quiet and unsupervised
afternoon catching fish. As Maupassant notes, possibly with a
trace of envy himself, 'The kindly sun warmed their backs; they
heard nothing and thought of nothing; the rest of the world no
longer existed for them; they simply fished.'

At this point the Prussian artillery opens up. As the shells
thunder out of their hilltop cannons and swish overhead, maim-
ing, murdering and pulverizing unknown civilians a few miles
away, it occurs to Morissot and Sauvage that they have been
lolling through the afternoon in a sort of war-evacuated No Man's
Land, beyond the reach of all governments, including their own,
in a rare and complete condition of liberty unfamiliar to nearly
all the world's populations, which are condemned to reside in
some political state or other:

[Morissot] was suddenly filled with a peace-loving man's anger at these madmen who insisted on fighting one another, and he growled: 'They must be fools, killing each other like that.'

'They're worse than wild beasts,' said Monsieur Sauvage.

And Morissot, who had just hooked a bleak, declared: 'To think that it'll always be like that as long as we have governments!'

Monsieur Sauvage corrected him: 'The Republic would never have declared war. ...'

'With kings,' Morissot broke in, 'you have war abroad; with republics, you have war at home.'

They started a friendly argument, discussing the great political problems with the sweet reasonableness of peaceful men of limited intelligence, and agreeing on one point: that men would never be free.

Their own freedom, too, is not to last. Practically as they speak, they find themselves surrounded by Prussian soldiers, who turn out to have been watching them all the while – even their afternoon's liberty seems to have been only an illusion – and hustled off to a Prussian outpost.

At once, they are confronted with a choice between the guilt of treason and execution.

The Prussian officer in charge, 'a hairy giant of a man', informs them 'in excellent French' that they must either tell him the password that will permit them to return through the French lines (which he surmises that they must have been told) or be shot: 'Nobody will be any the wiser. You will go back as if nothing had happened, and the secret will go with you. If you refuse you die – you die on the spot. Now choose.'

The reader comes quickly to understand that the officer has no particular desire to kill them – he is no evil-minded sadist – but is himself the new type of gelid military bureaucrat common to many armies these days. It is not killing that he enjoys. In fact killing means nothing to him. It is getting information. One cannot imagine him weeping over a human death. He might become ill, however, and require hospitalization, over a mislaid telegram. His arrogance derives from his abstractness. He is unconnected to society except through his career, and is divorced from life, existing at a modern suburban distance from human conflicts.

Morissot and Sauvage, however, can make nothing of his request. They are simple, straightforward people as Maupassant describes them, and the very idea of cooperating in the act of guilty betrayal proposed by the officer is unintelligible if not mysterious to them.

The officer is himself puzzled by what he misinterprets as their stubbornness, but he persists, even drawing aside first the one and then the other, in a vain attempt to lure each of the two friends into telling him the password and saving his own life. He gets nowhere. Neither of the two is willing to say anything. In the end, the by-now nonplussed officer orders a firing squad to form up, and as Morissot and Sauvage embrace each other for the last time, he has them shot. He orders their bodies, weighted with stones, to be tossed into the river where they have been fishing, and the fish that they have caught to be turned over to the company cook to be fried for dinner.

Throughout these miserable final events, and echoing as an after-effect of the story's grisly end, the reader is conscious not simply of a clash between two countries, but of two incompatible understandings of civilization itself, indeed of a clash between two eras of guilt and freedom. What becomes clear is that Morissot and Sauvage are put to death because they cannot comprehend the modern world and its coldly insistent rule-making and guilt-production. They are killed, in other words, not merely for their unwillingness to divulge a password and betray their country but for their assertion of an old-fashioned human pleasure, the peaceful, once free option of going fishing.

II

The History of Guilt

1. Guilt as a Divine Gift

Guilt becomes fashionable for modern people through the old agrarian religions: Judaism, Christianity and Mohammedanism. These religions, whatever their beauties and possible truths, emerge from the rural earth, from deserts and mountains as much as from spiritual discoveries and impulses. They have nothing to do with cities, except as cities become witnesses to the encroachments of crimes and sin. These, then, are the religions of crops and livestock, of sweaty animal sacrifices, of harsh divine-ordered treks and of magical military expeditions. Betrayal centres on the land or on wars fought over land. Salvations are rescues from the perils and hardships of nature. Everything is concrete and rocky. The universe, like the earth, is finite. Populations are small. Even Adam and Eve's disobedience consists not simply of the breaking of a divine edict but also of the violation of a garden, of a tree and of paradisal soil. One of its results is that the human inhabitants of Eden are expelled and forced to live as best they can off the less welcoming soil of the real world.

The histories of Judaism and Christianity are in many ways made up of similar and contrary reactions to the dour assumption, if not presumption, of Adam and Eve's primal guilt. These histories are by no means smooth, and within each religion are to be found sets of wholly disparate responses, and variations on them, to the idea of this human couple's misbehaviour. Nonetheless, a few generalizations and distinctions can readily be made.

First, neither Jews nor Christians talk much about guilt in the primal sense until they reach their theological periods, as these may be termed, when rabbis and priests, respectively, begin to provide running commentaries on biblical passages. The Book of Genesis, in its chapters that supposedly deal with this type of guilt, never uses the word. For Jews, the theological period begins as a written exercise in approximately the fourth century; for Christians, it starts with St Augustine in the fifth century. In each case the commentaries and controversies (in Hebrew, *midrashim*) then continue in a sort of headlong flight, as if lit by a novel, institutional enthusiasm, straight into modern times.

Second, the fact that the question of Original Sin, or inherent guilt, is taken up only at a relatively late stage of both religions is probably revealing. It suggests that the concept may not have mattered a great deal, or even have been known, to early Jews and Christians.

Original Sin is nonetheless connected by each religion to 'Man's first disobedience', as Milton puts it in *Paradise Lost*. This involved Adam and Eve's eating of the tree of knowledge of good and evil in the Garden of Eden (Genesis 3). Plucking the fruit of this tree, and eating it, had been expressly forbidden by God, and when Adam and Eve did so anyway, having been lured into their act of defiance by 'the serpent' (Satan is not mentioned; later theological doctrine proposes that the serpent is Satan), who assured them that they would 'not surely die' if they plunged ahead, God immediately punished them by ordering them to leave the garden.

They were also punished in other ways. Eve, whose name means 'the mother of all things living', was told that she would suffer distress when giving birth, that she would henceforth serve her husband Adam as his inferior, and that she and her female descendants would forever harbour an intense dislike of snakes (the serpent who tempted her was translated by God into a snake as part of his punishment). Adam was consigned to eternal toil. He had to scrape the earth for a living, and was informed by God that he would find it endlessly resistant, stony and unproductive. Both Eve and Adam were told that they would eventually die (nonetheless they lived on for hundreds of years). In fact the reason given by God for expelling them from Eden seems to have had only an indirect relation to their disobedience. God feared that they would next seek to become immortal, by moving on to eating of the tree of life. This could not be permitted, lest they became divine in more than their knowledge of good and evil. They were thus expelled from Eden for some anticipated disobedience which could never have taken place.

Few Jewish and all significant Christian interpretations presume Adam's fall (Eve's is counted as less momentous). Since Adam is presumed to be the first man, whether actually or symbolically, humanity itself is regarded as fallen. Several features of his Fall are accepted by influential commentators and are crucial to understanding its impact on Jews and Christians. Pre-eminent among these is that, especially among Christians, it is a permanent condition. It may eventually be redeemed by a messiah, or a day of judgement, or both, but in the meantime all human beings are born into a state of automatic, irrefutable guilt. Adam's disobedience is thus a uniquely consequential act whose results are quasi-biologically transferred from one generation to the next. Its uniqueness also lies in its terrible ambition. This consisted not merely in Adam and Eve's disobedience but in their goal of becoming 'like the gods' in knowledge, according to the serpent, or like God. A similar ambition, and act, with similarly unpleasant, long-term results, is depicted in the Tower of Babel story (Genesis 11). Humanity's punishment for building this tower, which was intended to reach as high as heaven and so to disturb God's dominion, was the confounding of its one language into many languages, and the scattering of its peoples into numerous disputatious tribes.

If reactions to these biblical tales of defiant ambition, divine punishment and human guilt among the Jewish and Christian commentators consort only flimsily with each other, they in turn vary drastically from the Moslem ones. In Islam, while the doctrine of Original Sin is known, because the Koran (revealed to Mohammed at Mecca in 651-52) is itself heavily dependent on biblical texts, it exercises no real influence and is rejected. This is because mankind is not perceived as requiring a redeemer. Christ is embraced as a prophet rather than a messiah, and is not viewed either as the son of God or as releasing, or needing to release, the human race from a condition of irremediable sin, or guilt, in some primordial sense.

Other types of unavoidable sin, or *kabira*, nonetheless become important within Islamic religious law, and committing *kabira* can prevent the sinner from gaining admission to Paradise. Since most people sin anyway, the laws governing *kabira*, together with the guilt-fostering frustrations that they inspire, often provoke mockery, as they sometimes do among religious Jews and Christians. Medieval Moslem poets, such as Abu Nuwas (d. 810), produce drinking songs, for instance, that celebrate the prohibited pleasures of wine: 'Come, my lord, let us rebel against the Despot of Heaven'; 'My proud soul will be content with nothing but the forbidden./I do not care when my cup of death will come;/I have already had my fill of the joys of the [wine] cup' (Andras Hamori trans.). Nuwas' bibulous, though genuine and risky defiance of God, or Allah, is hardly comparable, however, to the Judeo-Christian primal torment.

It also scarcely resembles the primordial conviction of guilt that shoulders through the much earlier Sumerian creation-poetry (from the Ur III dynasty, 2112-2004 BC), in which the hero-god Marduk is described as having triumphed over an evil dragon, Ti'mat, who is also a female mythical symbol of the salt sea. Despite her defeat, the Sumerian dragon's devil offspring continue to beset mankind, using disease as their weapon. Disease itself was apparently regarded by the Sumerians as a punishment for having sinned against the gods, and so as a signal of human guilt. A variation of this attitude made its way into the European Middle Ages, when lepers, as well as the mentally retarded and physically deformed, were considered guilty sinners whose diseased state indicated hidden defiance and divine retribution.

Hinduism, by contrast, like its offshoot, Buddhism, shows no interest in spontaneous guilt. It abjures the possibility of disorders in nature. It treats as error the notion that any type of divine arrangement of phenomena can be threatened by human beings. The realms of the blessed are indifferent to mortal strife. Enlightened souls have risen above ethical conflicts through devotion.

As a four-thousand-year synthesis of Indian religious thought and religious principles disseminated across the Asian sub-continent by Aryans (*c.* 1500 BC), Hindu philosophy culminates in the sensual and literary brilliance of the *Upanishads*. These magnificent poems stress the premise that the Self is identical with the individual soul in an absolute reality. The *Upanishads'* focus is on a universe that engages in endless birth and dissolution, and on the individual's emancipation from desire, or the tortures of *samsara*, with psychic liberation enabling the person who achieves it to enjoy the blessings of *nirvana*. Though Shiva, the destroyer god of the Hindu trinity, implies among Hindus a consciousness of grotesque evil (the other two chief divinities are Brahma, the creator, and Vishnu, the preserver), unremitting human guilt of any sort is nowhere asserted. Instead, rather like the biblical 'Song of Songs', Hindu poetry, as in the twelfth-century 'Gita Govinda' of Jayadeva, presents a refreshed spiritual sensuality according to which Krishna, an avatar of Vishnu, can be greeted as a lover (in contrast to the 'Song of Songs' itself, which is spiritual only by inference):

Sandal and garment of yellow and lotus garlands upon his
   body of blue,
In his dance the jewels of his ears in movement dangling
   over his smiling cheeks.
Hari [Krishna] disports himself with charming women
   given to love!

The wife of a certain herdsman sings as Hari sounds a tune
   of love
Embracing him all the while with all the force of her full and
   swelling breasts.
Hari here disports himself with charming women given to
   love. (George Keyt trans.)

The Hindu perception of the universe, in other words, and of human relations within it, is fundamentally positive. Human disobedience and guilt play no part in the harmony of its universal cyclical repetitions.

In the light of these diverse attitudes, the history of religious guilt may broadly be understood as erratic, if not sibylline. Divinely prepared guilt appears and vanishes. It satisfies a cultural mood for a time, then subsides. It has rooted itself stoutly over centuries, for example, among the Piaroa Amerindians of Venezuela, whose notions of communal guilt and communal expiation are still associated with sin, evil, filth, disease and madness – with disruptions both of a cosmic order and an individual's righteousness. Piaroans are trained to avoid this unhappiness from the age of six. They are able to do so, if often with difficulty, because of the collective pressures of other Piaroans.

Behind these exertions, though, and those of dissimilar guilt-laden cultures, lies the hint that climate and geography play important roles in the stimulation of many feelings of extreme spiritual unworthiness, or of *a priori* guilt. Tropical rainforests, like stormy mountain tops, may present conditions harsh enough to buttress beliefs in lurking (though expiable) human wickedness. Temperate climates, on the other hand, seem to inherit these ideas but not to produce them. Urban cultures appear to expand on them, and seriously to modify them, but seldom to invent them. Climate is not all, of course, any more than Edgar's belief in *King Lear* that 'ripeness is all'. It is probably more than coincidentally linked, however, to nightmares of universal damnation. The sense of a dooming, fangy guilt, along with the promise of divine salvation, seems to develop most bitterly amidst a feral terrain and fierce animal life, or in an erased landscape. Nostalgia for a sacrificed paradisal garden, after all, tallies as more poignant when pitched against the skin-baking terror of desert sands and scalding skies. These may easily send shivers of intrinsic unworthiness down the spines of men and women who find their relations with the larger cosmos, and the divine, wrenching and precarious in any case.

A temperate climate may also have something to do with the unsympathetic attitude of the pagan cultures of ancient Greece and Rome toward concepts of primal guilt. Softer, more lucid sunlight may mollify the demons of the human heart. Oedipus thus appears as an influential anomaly. Vaguely like Christ, he becomes a scapegoat for the sickness of his community, the city of Thebes, which has contracted the plague, and which, according to ancient political doctrines, is entitled to hold him responsible as its king for its withering affliction.

While the Oedipus story exercises an indirect influence on important later Western legends of a guilty wasteland, in which conventionally an entire population sickens according to the taboo-breaking crimes of its ruler, the story scarcely reflects the common pagan indifference to primal guilt. This indifference, or ignorance, is revealed in the coolish lyrics of ancient Roman epitaphs, which seem deeply moving in their acceptance of the absolute loss of a beloved:

Stranger, my message is short. Stand by and read it through. Here is the unlovely tomb of a lovely woman. Her parents called her Claudia by name. She loved her husband with her whole heart. She bore two sons; of these she leaves one on earth; under the earth she has placed the other. She was charming in converse, yet proper in bearing. She kept house, she made wool. That's my last word. Go your way. (135-120 BC, Rome; E.H. Warmington trans.)

Marcus Statius Chilo, freedman of Marcus, lies here. Ah! Weary wayfarer, you there who are passing by me, though you may walk as long as you like, yet here's the place you must come to: frontage 10 ft, depth 10 ft. (Early first century BC, near Cremona; E.H. Warmington trans.)

Hail! Herennia Crocine, dear to her own, is shut up in this tomb, Crocine dear to her own. My life is over; other girls too have lived their lives and died before me. Enough now. May the reader say as he departs, 'Crocine, lightly rest the earth on you.' Farewell to all you above ground. (First century BC, Spain; E.H. Warmington trans.)

The sadness in these cases, which are typical, is unmingled with guilt and ideas of salvation. It is a sadness born of simple facts and is devoid of dreams of any sort of future.

It would be a mistake, however, to excuse the ancient Greeks and Romans, and particularly the ancient Greeks, from all notions of guilty divine remonstrance. The world of the Acropolis and of shining, ruined temples conceals its own poisoned chalice. The collection of beliefs known today as paganism, whose original meaning is 'a landmark fixed in the earth', always included more than crowds of lascivious, eloquent gods and goddesses, charming nymphs and prostrating, imaginative feasts – as these are depicted, for example, in Hesiod's *Theogony*, in surviving fragments of Petronius' first-century novel *Satyricon*, in Longus' *Daphnis and Chloe* (Greek, second or third century) and in Cicero's *On the Nature of the Gods*. Ancient Greek and Roman folk worship develops over many centuries. Its growth, like that of other religions, is twisty and contradictory. Older attitudes, such as appear in Roman epitaphs, continue to blossom alongside newer, ferocious ones.

Chameleon beliefs about Hades, for instance, which is not to be confused with the Christian Hell, though the pagan influence on it is considerable, seem to form a valuable index to shifting pagan ideas of guilt. Homer's Hades (*c*. ninth century BC) is fairly innocuous. The ghosts that Odysseus encounters among its cold aisles are hapless, pale reflections of their former bodies. They are powerless as well, even if some of them seem able to foretell the future. The only guilty sinners whom Odysseus discovers in Hades are not human at all but mythical enemies of the gods, tormented beings such as Tantalus and Sisyphus, who were punished in the upper world and subsequently transferred to the lower, there to be left languishing or kept busy at pointless, humiliating tasks.

By the fifth century BC, however, Hades had changed for many Greeks into a more dangerous place. Plato in his *Cratylus* draws attention to the premise of the newer Orphic cults, according to which the soul is immortal, but the body is its prison. One upshot of this degraded view of the body, which is later to have a major impact on Christian convictions, is that an afterlife in Hades must now be understood as possibly punitive. If sinners in this life have not performed the prescribed Orphic rites of purification, in Hades they 'will lie in the mud' and be condemned to repeat forever their impure earthly behaviour as their punishment. The mythical ferryboatman Charon, who escorts the souls of the dead across the River Styx to their final abode, is thus transformed from a mild underworld bureaucrat into a grisly usher into a house of torture.

The Orphic innovation itself evidently came about in response to a change in Athenian law. For centuries it had been maintained that a criminal's family and their descendants ought to bear the onus of his crimes, paying for them continuously through an indefinitely stigmatized future, precisely as if they themselves were criminals. The sins of the fathers were horribly visited on succeeding generations. In the seventh century BC, however, the Athenian law-giver Solon argued that this custom lacked good sense and compassion, and, with commendable modernity, that any punishment ought properly to be directed at the criminal alone. As Solon's legal revision won acceptance, the Orphic belief in a retributive Hades picked up authority among people who felt that the next world might deal better with that enormous class of sinners and criminals who had managed to get off scot free in this one.

The historian Herodotus (fifth century BC) refers to yet another pagan shift in attitudes toward guilt. He identifies a guilt-fascination among the Eleusinian cults at Athens, which he considers an import from Egypt. Herodotus associates this type of guilt with ancient forms of Egyptian Osiris worship and with Egyptian pacts and prayers to appease the ever-present, hovering and insatiable souls of mummified ancestors. These ghostly figures were said to require daily nourishment in the form of tomb-deposited food and costly sacrifices. In Plato's *Apology*, Socrates makes clear his scepticism about these elaborate needs of the dead, and wonders whether embalmed corpses can require anything at all. His philosophical curiosity stimulated meagre agreement. By Plato's day Eleusinian-inspired rumours that Hades was a place of reward, in the Fields of Elysium, and punishment, in its other frigid zones, circulated widely, and initiation into the Eleusinian mysteries, which were based on rites of obeisance to Demeter and Persephone at Eleusis, had become part of Athens' public religion.

Even for those who may have raised a socratic eyebrow at these ceremonies, which many seem to have undertaken half in belief, half in disbelief, they offered at least 'good hopes' of a pleasant, guilt-purged afterlife in a Hades that looked more and more like a place to which they must come for a final reckoning with their guilty offences both against brazen ancestors and the discontented gods.

2. Judeo-Christian Divergences

Jewish and Christian reactions to feelings of primal and other types of unworthiness flow into geographically skewed, separate valleys. Hebrew has over twenty words for sin, possibly more than any other language. At the very least, this indicates an interest in guilt. Three words are crucial. In Leviticus, the reader is told of *het*, or innocent sin; of *avon*, or deliberate sin; and of *pesha*, or the kind of sin that, whether innocent or deliberate, amounts to rebellion against God.

All three types require that bullocks, lambs and goats be sacrificed to appease God's wrath and effect atonement. Only *pesha*, however, the sin of rebelliousness against God, may be said to qualify as guilt-producing in the strict sense of the word. *Het* and *avon* refer to largely social violations. These may provoke shame, regret and embarrassment. They may refer to several types of criminal guilt. They may be included in *pesha*. Absent from them, however, are the mysterious dimensions of cosmic insolence such as appear in Adam's eating of the tree of the knowledge of good and evil and in the Tower of Babel story. Neither *het* nor *avon* necessarily involves a darker transgression against the divine values of worship, respect for God's commandments, holding true to one's pacts or covenants with God and above all keeping the one God of all things created as one's only God. The ferocity of God's injunction against idolatry is unmistakable, both in the first and the third Commandments: 'Thou shalt have no other gods before Me', and 'Thou shalt not take the name of the Lord thy God in vain; for the Lord will not hold him guiltless that taketh his name in vain' (Deuteronomy, 5).

What is clear from the Hebrew plethora of terms for sin, and often by extension of guilt of this God-insulting type, is that for religious Jews guilt is traditionally less a part of the social cement than it is a tendril of the divine connection. It preserves an attachment to God and a perverse allegiance to divine power, much as any magnetic negative is attracted to a magnetic positive. In this sense, guilt may be understood as partly defining the traditionally religious Jew's human condition and cosmic relationship.

Rabbinical Judaism, no doubt as a consequence, exhibits an avid interest in unavoidable guilt. It accepts as a given that everyone without exception will behave guiltily, incurring God's wrath and requiring repentance. On the other hand, the doctrine of Original Sin remains undiscussed and is thus in fact not accepted. One might easily argue that from a rabbinical point of view the doctrine is unnecessary or supererogatory. If sins of all three types are universal, then rebellion against God must also be universal. Wrestlings with God, as when Jacob wrestled with an unknown adversary till dawn, only to discover that he had been wrestling with God, must figure mightily into all true belief, and Adam's Fall must therefore be understood as in some fashion recurring in each human life.

As a result, there should be no practical difference between the rabbinical position and Christian theological arguments in favour of Original Sin. This is not the case, however, and an actual if not a practical difference exists. It lies in the fact that rabbinical Judaism has always maintained that no one is born into a condition of guilt. All guilt, or defiance of God, is a matter of choice. Free will plays a role in each instance of *pesha*. While this attitude must be encouraging to those who are convinced of a fundamental human rationality, or at least of a basic difference between human beings and machines, it only complicates the meaning of Adam and Eve's defiance in Eden. Adam's Fall must ultimately be understood as a useless warning against an unavoidable catastrophe.

The rabbinical attitude is itself rejected by influential Jewish mystical cults, starting in the Middle Ages. Gershom Scholem (in *Major Trends in Jewish Mysticism*) discovers a definite enthusiasm for versions of the doctrine of Original Sin among the

followers of the Lurianic *Kabbalah* (by Isaac Luria, early sixteenth century) and the *Zohar* (by Moses de Leon, thirteenth
century, but attributed to Simon ben Yohai, second century). The
author of the *Zohar* argues that evil came into the world not
through Adam's Fall but through predestination. Evil is built
into reality, as a type of dross within life itself (this was also the
belief of the Christian Gnostics). Human guilt is thus intrinsic
and somehow a consequence of biology. Scholem points out that
the greater influence of the idea of Original Sin on mystical
Jewish groups than on rabbinical Judaism can be traced to the
correspondingly greater influence on them of the experience of
exile. The Fall of Adam is construed as reflected in the two-thou-
sand-year separation of the Jewish people from their homeland.

　　The Christian history of guilt is by contrast less abstract, more
personal and more doom-struck or apocalyptic. Throughout the
Middle Ages, clerical thought, among heretics and orthodox
alike, continues to proclaim the deepest possible suspicion and
condemnation of sensual experience, of all sensual experience,
discovering fresh and frightening sources of guilt in the decep-
tions, as they are regarded, of the five senses and the inherent
pollution of the human body. Traditional Christian ideas of guilt
are planted with St Augustine's *Confessions*, and nourished
through his immensely compelling other books, *The City of God*,
On Christian Doctrine and *The Enchiridion on Faith, Hope and
Love*. These are themselves in part responses to such biblical
texts as St Paul's epistles to the Galatians, Ephesians, Philip-
pians, Thessalonians, Timothy and Hebrews. It should at once be
stressed, however, that despite an unending stream of theological denunciations of the flesh as permanently guilty, various
medieval Christian cultures, especially those of England,
France, Italy, Germany and Austria, produce lyric poetry, epics
and romances during the High Middle Ages that are among the
most lavishly sensual, often especially in the sexual sense, of any
in the history of literature. All interesting cultures are paradoxes, and guilt itself is often as much a vitamin for sublime
creation as for wintry depression.

　　If of St Paul it may be said, to borrow a phrase from Ben
Jonson, that 'where guilt is, rage and courage doth abound', of St

Augustine it may easily be added, to cite a line from the Roman moralist Publius Syrius (first century BC), 'How unhappy is he who cannot forgive himself.'

For Augustine the weak membranes of life seemed everywhere to burst open with showers of guilt. One is reminded of Kafka's wound. Certainly no one has ever shown a more punishing awareness of the possibilities of guilt in himself or others. In modern times such extreme awareness would be called pathology. In Augustine's day, and for over a thousand years thereafter, it was understood as holiness. No doubt it is presumptuous to reduce the awareness of one age to the ideas of pathology of another. In Augustine's case this would also mean overlooking his brilliance, his commitment to truth, which later assumed harsh proportions, and his insights into the suffering of the guilty.

It was not always so for him. As an adolescent and then a young man in Carthage, he led a notoriously loose life. 'I loved to love, and out of a deep-seated want, I hated myself for wanting not,' he writes, with a self-admonitory clarity suggestive of Dostoyevski's Stavrogin over a dozen centuries later. Immediately, and characteristically, he adds, 'I defiled, therefore, the spring of friendship with the filth of concupiscence, and I beclouded its brightness with the hell of lustfulness' (*Confessions*, bk. III, ch. 1). Such sentiments point to a temperament as capable of defiance as contrition, as full of truculence as remorse, but unknown to Augustine are Stavrogin's alienation from God and a world of spiritless materialism. A profound sense of sin, which Augustine is among the first to identify as the source of guilt, haunts him amidst his pleasures.

He seems as well fairly early to have arrived at his dislike, if not hatred, of lust, detecting an imaginary horror in what he regarded as its erasure of free will and rationality. On the other hand, sin itself emanates, he argues (in *The City of God*), from the soul rather than lust or the body. Were it not for God's mercy, Adam's guilty disobedience would have led to the death of the entire human race, presumably before it got decently started. Adam, who is held more to task than Eve, could have refused to eat the Edenic apple, but his choosing to eat it introduced corruption, and the inherited likelihood of eternal tortures in Hell, into all succeeding generations. Everyone, including unbaptised babies, is guilty (a doctrine rejected by the Church itself since the time of Calvin).

It is not unfair to say that nearly all of Augustine's writings, which were composed after his conversion to Christianity, are suffused both with great beauty and fierce, intemperate guilt. Whether one accepts his doctrine or not, one cannot also but acknowledge the accuracy of his insights into the problem of human unworthiness before an awesome and inexplicable divinity. Augustine is constantly aware that while there are clearly various types of guilt, ranging from the primal or built-in to the social and criminal, the antiquity of the evidence reveals that guilt itself is one of the oldest emotions or states of mind, always combining elements of ritual and murderousness. He accepts that guilt must always hover nearby slaughter. It must linger over bloodthirstiness and annihilation. The annihilation may be mental, an excruciating torment leading even into a groping lunacy, but around it and often within it must inevitably blossom the threat of actual killing. This gruelling fact, as he seems to have understood better than almost anyone, also exposes guilt's paradox (a paradox not unlike the paradoxes of medieval European cultures): its creative power, stimulated by the desire to escape its twilights, darknesses and venomousness. Many of the loftiest moments of human existence, including large numbers of its bravest acts of love, are thus, as his view of God's grace implies, unexpected vessels bustling across the barbed waves of an ocean of guilt. Their beauty is the more exciting for its grim source.

In Augustine's delicious, terrible phrases, one races down to the sallow shores of embarrassment, shame and regret from hills of joy and acceptance, before Adam's Fall, coming at last upon this gloomy ocean of guilt. Ships and boats are available, or one can build one's own, thanks to God's grace, and one may embark freely upon the spreading waters. One's journey is expensive, and for nearly everyone (except the elect, who sail safely onward to Heaven) disastrous. On the other hand, the hounds of accusation and self-accusation crouch at one's heels, and their mercilessness, should one fail to embark post-haste, allows the grey waves before one, with their inconsolable melancholy, to seem unthreatening by comparison: better misery than ruthlessness.

Yet the beefy ruthlessness of this ocean itself is barely concealed. It is, among other things, an ocean of memory. Once one is embarked and launched, the sky darkens and furious tempests born of one's own and Eden's past assail one on all sides. If, for example, one is tempted into sex for pleasure instead of procreation, and this in marriage alone, one has yielded to the blotting sin that Augustine and his clerical successors proscribe as blushing forth from Adam's Fall: 'concupiscence', which he seems himself to have enjoyed, and then spurned, in his Carthage days. Any rushing away from social disgrace leads bitterly and only into disgrace before God.

On no account, however, can Augustine be held responsible for the excesses to which the misuse of his doctrine of universal guilt often gave way: the Inquisition, begun under Pope Gregory IX in the thirteenth century, with its fusillade of death sentences fired off at supposedly guilty witches and heretics, its own guilty mayhem of rack-stretched and smoking bodies; the self-accusing Flagellants, in the fourteenth century, whose pious, violent parades through scores of European towns and villages appalled the inhabitants and seduced thousands of lost souls into joining their descent into resignation and sickening self-punishments; and the promiscuous growth throughout Europe, but with special virulence from the fourteenth century onwards, of anti-semitism. What seems clear, though, is that following Augustine, the concept of primal guilt, and more specifically of Original Sin, was welcomed across North Africa and Europe by masses of people. Many, like Augustine himself, were formerly non-Christians.

It was perhaps only to be expected that those who now believed themselves to be automatically guilty in the Augustinian sense should assign a collective guilt to their biblical predecessors, the Jews. The sweeping character of their additional accusations levelled at Jews, however, beyond the monstrous traditional one that all Jews were 'Christ-killers', together with the popular and nauseating hysteria that surrounded these accusations, often leading straight into genocidal pogroms, could probably not have been anticipated. Thus throughout the High Middle Ages and thereafter, Jews were routinely described as guilty of usury, bribery, murder, sorcery, human sacrifice, cannibalism and poisoning wells to spread the plague. Isolating Jews in ghettos, owning them and killing them became socially acceptable. The gold and cream-coloured cathedrals of Russia, Germany, France and England frequently turned into nests of bigotry and hatred. Christian piety was often accompanied by tawdry slaughter.

It is, moreover, an irony of history that the very people, the Jews, who had themselves rejected the possibility of collective guilt, should be marked out for it. It is a further irony that in the twentieth century the German people, who under the Nazis assented in one way or another to the collective annihilation of millions of Jews, should themselves be confronted with the accusation of collective guilt for having done so. To say this is not to urge that the German people are indeed collectively guilty of genocide. Anyone who believes in human free will can find in such a charge only the crudest hypocrisy. The accusation persists, however, and seems to have a life of its own, playing its dire, ghostly role in the history of guilt. It echoes eerily in the words of the Nazi war criminal Hans Frank before he was hanged at Nuremberg in 1946 (as governor of occupied Warsaw, Frank was convicted of organizing the mass-starvation of Jews in the ghetto there): 'A thousand years will pass and the guilt of Germany will not be erased.' Along these lines, it is worth noting that a complete repudiation by the Church of the accusation of collective Jewish guilt for the crucifixion of Christ was offered only close to two thousand years after the fact.

Caustic reactions to all this Augustinian-inspired guilt could indeed, and easily, have been anticipated, though – if only because medieval Catholicism was itself a drastic reaction to pagan decadence. In the sixteenth century, the newly developing Reformation caught fire as a flight, if not escape, from the older Augustinian ideas of Original Sin. It battened especially on an infectious revulsion with primal guilt. Large numbers of people suddenly seemed to find the Augustinian castigation of humanity unbearable, if not also implausible.

Superb translations of the Bible, by Martin Luther in Germany (1521), by William Tyndale (1534) and his successors with the King James Bible (1611) in England (though Tyndale, threatened with death, was forced to publish in Belgium), now sought to release Christians from medieval Church theology by returning them to the sacred texts of Christianity, doing so in ordinary speech that everybody could understand. The polished, yet often oppressive and obscure expositions of the Church were to be eliminated. Direct contact with the divine was to be restored. The divine voice was to be heard once again in its pristine clarity.

A problem arose, though, in that, as scholastics such as Thomas Aquinas (d. 1274) had previously contended, the divine meaning or voice had in fact never been terribly clear. At the least its lucidity for one group seemed almost at once to amount to confusion for the next. Squabbles immediately erupted. Sects proliferated. Supposedly 'literal' readings of the Bible replaced theological commentaries, only very soon themselves to exercise a control over worshippers as rigid as any previously imposed by the thousands of musty, old-fashioned priests. Everyone had his own favourite 'literal' reading, and those of Lutherans, Puritans, Presbyters, Quakers, Shakers, Mennonites, Remonstrants and other Protestants scarcely agreed with one another, especially on the transcendent problem of Adam's guilty Fall and humanity's guilt after that. A sloughing off of the Augustinian guilty skin seemed only to expose another one equally wrinkled.

In this jumbled predicament, it was ironically Augustine who had the last word. He had often claimed that biblical texts had been deprived of their full sense through repeated translations. It could be restored only by the devotional good intentions of readers. More than this, the intentional cloudiness of many biblical passages ought to prompt an ever-eager quest for truth. This is what now happened, though not perhaps in the way that Augustine had hoped. Modern philosophy was born, and out of it, as well as out of a search for an understanding both of the Bible and of mythology in terms of the states of mind embodied in them, modern psychology: each a discipline devoted if not to spiritual truth, then at least to a sensitivity to language, and beyond this, to interpretation. The Reformation thus eventually led into secular accounts of guilt.

3. Psychology and Guilt

As a thinker, and perhaps especially about guilt, Sigmund Freud (1856-1939) makes the same reductionist mistake as Karl Marx (1818-83), that of asking a single rickety bridge to bear the full weight of humanity. It cannot, and eventually collapses. With Marx the bridge is economics: it alone accounts for human history and behaviour. With Freud it is psychopathology.

As a result, one finds in his theories of culture and individual development a type of fenced-in brilliance. The natural animals of human instinct, together with the entire menagerie of human emotions, are not let out of their cages. Their keeper also insists that their activities in the wild must be exactly the same as what we see them doing in captivity. This type of assumption works well in the hard sciences of physics, chemistry and biology. If one extracts masking impurities, for instance, fluorite and several other minerals will display a grand luminescence when irradiated in the laboratory by appropriate wave-lengths of ultraviolet light. The same phenomenon can then be observed if these minerals are exposed to ordinary daylight, which contains minute amounts of ultraviolet. The unknowns in this kind of controlled situation are comparatively few, however, and it remains problematic whether a mass murderer examined by a psychiatrist will display the same behaviour in his office as he might somewhere else.

From the point of view of the history of guilt of all types, Freud's great contribution is his assertion of the independence and utter secrecy of the unconscious. In proposing that it is a purely mechanical and hidden portion of the mind, or as materialists wish to have it, the brain, he severs the unconscious from volition. The unconscious is a device, and possibly a linguistic device, no more. The effect of Freud's theory is that no one can any longer be assigned responsibility for his or her dreams, nightmares, moments of reverie and the sudden, often furious thoughts that may enter the conscious mind without warning.

So enormous has been the influence of this idea, and so widespread its acceptance, to the point that most educated people today simply take it for granted, that one finds it almost impossible now to appreciate how astonishing it seemed when it was first proposed, or what storms of resentment and sighs of relief it loosed across the world. Suffice it that this idea quite by itself introduced a complete revision into how masses of human beings understood themselves, one as drastic as the new notion of the physicists that people were simply a set of radio waves (some would naturally add, 'But what remarkable radio waves!').

This was because it had always been asssumed, and maintained by the Church and many Protestant sects, that each person's thoughts were without question the result of his or her character. As character was taken to include ethical choices, all mental activities, no matter how squeamish and cloistered, revealed the true state of anyone's integrity and corruption. People everywhere could thus indeed be held responsible for their thoughts, dreams and nightmares. They might sin while asleep or while musing in a chair. No distinction was made between thought and deed, and the sin of lust, for example, or murder, could incur as much guilt if committed mentally as physically. Imaginary sex or murder was, and for traditional believers still is, as guilt-infected as real sex or real murder. (It may be presumed that advocates of so ridiculous a doctrine had little experience of sex, and had never witnessed a murder.)

In proposing the independence of the unconscious from volition, Freud consigned this religious view to the dustbin of psychological curiosities. It soon came to be broadly regarded as a superstition. This in turn released vast numbers of people from the burden of many sorts of religious guilt.

A further implication was even more threatening to established religion: all of the guilty assumptions about humanity of Judaism and Christianity might now be subjected to psychological analysis, and both religions stripped down to a skeleton of purely neurotic and other psychological dramas. Devils, giants, the monsters of Hell, the abandoned and betrayed garden, the ghastly indictment of the Cross, the idea of the messiah or of Christ as the Redeemer of human sins and primordial guilt, and even the sanguinary, divine sacrifice – every one of these ancient enchantments might be shown to be a mere tragic symbol in an unexposed mental theatre of buried rituals, fears of nature and infantile emotional struggles. Religion itself might be revealed as no more than what William Cowper calls a 'guilty splendour' (*The Task*, bk. III (1785)), or what Nathaniel Hawthorne describes in 'Young Goodman Brown' (1837) as a memory of a crime, in which we still 'exult to behold the whole earth one stain of guilt, one mighty blood spot'. Judaism and Christianity, which are above all historical religions, might thus be denied their historical-spiritual meanings and exposed as mere fossilized imitations of primitive stages of human grief and joy. Humanity's guilty relation to the universe would be seen to be insupportable.

Freud's onslaught slices knife-like through *Totem and Taboo* (1913), *The Acquisition and Control of Fire* (1932) and *Moses and Monotheism* (1939), with the latter completed in the last year of his life and now generally discredited because of its absurd claim that cultural characteristics, and specifically monotheistic beliefs, can be inherited. (In fairness to Freud, it must be said that he himself expressed reservations about this book.)

Freud's analysis of the relations between guilt and religion, and that of his successors, proceeds from two assumptions that are powerful, useful and questionable. The first is that Judaism, Christianity and other guilt-influenced religions, such as to some extent paganism, consist of allegories of hoary human conflicts whose true psychological depths are camouflaged by holy dogmas. The second is that these allegories, if understood in a purely psychological way, refer to an unconscious but coherent and real history of individual human strivings toward emotional freedom, and their frequent failure. What is culturally significant within each religion, therefore, is not at all its claim to sacred revelation, nor its pretension to spiritual truth, but an unmentioned and in fact previously unrecognized message, concealed among the lit candles, the sacred books, the prayers, the bowed heads, the chants, the splendid music, the acts of contrition, the murmured griefs, the miracles and the sweet blessings: an account of a mysterious mental illness and of healthy, violent battles with it.

A psychological saga of the human race can be separated from its religious trappings.

As early as 1907, Freud describes a connection between ceremonies of piety and obsessional neurosis (in 'Obsessive Actions and Religious Practices'). Hallowed rituals, like those of the obsessive neurotic, are self-protecting responses to the repression of partly sexual instincts. He adds that 'the formation of a religion, too, seems to be based on the suppression, the renunciation, of certain instinctual impulses'. In *Totem and Taboo*, the sufferings of a tragic hero such as Oedipus are presented as the 'tragic guilt' that results from rebellion 'against some divine or human authority': 'He had to suffer because he was the primal father, the Hero of the great primaeval tragedy which was being re-enacted with a tendentious twist; and the tragic guilt was the guilt which he had to take on himself in order to relieve the Chorus [or the people of Thebes] from theirs.' Oedipus' tragedy, moreover, is now to be grasped as precisely analogous to that of Christ on the cross. In *Moses and Monotheism* Freud adduces the hypothesis that the devout, Jews and Christians alike, seek to increase 'their own sense of guilt in order to stifle their doubts of God'. Judaism is seen as the 'father' religion, against which a murderous, guilty and Oedipal hatred is directed by Christians belonging to the religion of the son, or Christ, for whose guilty murder they feel responsible. Christianity is viewed as an advance over Judaism because Christians acknowledge this divine murder while Jews deny it. Any claim of an actual divine indebtedness or guilt is assumed to be fallacious, or an unsubstantiated error.

The potency of these and similar ideas, and their elaboration in various directions, often at odds with Freud, especially by Carl Jung (1875-1961), has always resided in their clarity. For the first time, the psychological and anthropological aspects of religion seemed analysable in a systematic way. Authors of genius, such as Shakespeare, and priestly sects, such as the Jesuits, had no doubt arrived at parallel insights into human psychology in the past. Their isolated data, though, had lacked the sort of empirical scientific organization that might expose long-range truths about the human species, and point the way to a mass therapeutic liberation from a religious prison. It must be conceded even by Freud's opponents that his hypotheses immediately resulted in formidable progress in comparative religion and anthropology, as well as in his freshly founded science of psychology itself.

Daunting questions also arose, however, almost from the start. How empirical was this science really? Did it account for all the relevant facts, or was it in important senses a simplification both of religion and human history?

For Jung, who had collaborated with Freud but parted company with him over his contention that all dreams were expressions of infantile sex-wishes, it seemed essential that any blueprint of religious history include the magnificent banqueting halls of spiritual feelings themselves. These, he argued, have a reality of their own and their own thrilling furnishings. They are not wholly or even partly explicable on the flimsy grounds of psychological needs, nor can they be collapsed into merely neurotic reactions to familial conflicts – as fantasies or consoling but somehow delusionary mirages.

Freud himself, it must be acknowledged, never denied the deeper possibilities of genuine spirituality, but insisted that the raw question whether God exists, and whether God is actually interested in stimulating humanity's primal guilt, have no place in a scientific inquiry. Instead, a human science ought to concern itself entirely with deterministic elucidations of human behaviour, and with the social illnesses that may be caused by pathology-induced superstitions. The psychological mechanisms that cause 'the formation of a religion' can thus be studied apart from its truth or falsity. As Jung did not accept this restrictive notion, the two most original of the seminal investigators of religious psychopathology somewhat huffily went their separate ways.

Jung's investigation of primordial religious guilt centres on four concepts, each of which also figures in the rest of his work: that of archetypes, that of individuation, that of the collective unconscious and (in the introduction to *Psychology and Alchemy*) that of the 'the abysmal contradictions of human nature', which, when confronted, lead 'to the possibility of a direct experience of light and darkness, of Christ and the devil'. The last of these concepts involves an experience of humanity's permanent and most fearful opposites, or 'antinomies'. This may or may not occur in any given life. There is no guarantee one way or the other. Neither intelligence nor education contributes to encountering its platinum revelation, and whether it happens is guided by 'fate'. The event can, however, be mightily assisted by an acceptance of the idea of Original Sin. To accept Original Sin is to open up 'the abyss of opposition in every individual', although even modestly intelligent people will probably carp at and reject its accompanying dogma and so shut themselves off from its terrifying beauty and its blinding though infinitely cleansing vision of the divine. The 'reality' of primordial guilt serves for Jung as a gateway to spiritual enlightenment.

The path to this gateway is marked by almost equally revelatory archetypal images. These are *a priori* universal designs and impressions, and actual buried memories, retained in the universal collective unconscious of the species. They are the residues of its first indelible adventures, or the beginnings of life itself, and they preserve, as in a capacious, planetary cinema, lost and ancient sacrifices, miraculous rescues, early storms, extinct beasts, antique flamings forth, hidden treasures and ultimate geometrical arrangements, magical-seeming ones, of divine creation. Paradoxically, it is only the highly 'individuated' man or woman, as Jung describes the evolved private sensibility, who is able consciously to recover these images, or patterns of God's presence, through dreams and nightmares, and through a consequent surrender to his or her spectral opposites. There is a spellbinding quality to Jung's ideas, whose truth remains as yet unestablished, and they represent in the strongest possible way, in modern times, a justification of the specifically Christian conception of primal guilt.

At all this the sceptic may only register surprise. Whether or not, as Marx once niggled, religion is the opiate of the people, dismissals of religion have become the morphine of many modern intellectuals. Bristling at prayer is as *de rigueur* as the railing of New-Age astrologers against the rational powers of science. In the eighteenth century Voltaire dryly observed that the god of religion must be a human invention. This is now often remarked with some heat. The reason is that in spite of scathing denunciations, the divine invention, if that is what it is, has neither weakened nor lost its value for many millions, large numbers of them intelligent and well educated.

Nor is the accusation levelled at them of religious naïveté an interesting one. There can be nothing naïve about spiritual guilt or awe. The innocent child's first astonished response to the vastness and intricacy of the universe is many an adult's final sophistication. Neither can the guilt that may accompany it be less than a twin of admiration. If religious forms of guilt have often descended into cruelties, these should perhaps also be understood as a natural albeit inexcusable response to the fact of ultimate human triviality, and perhaps as a rebellion of a horrid sort against humanity's cosmic insignificance.

III

The Rebellions against Guilt

1. Guilt as Oppression

It was only to be expected that if Adam and Eve were impertinent enough to defy God, their descendants would be sassy enough to reject any guilty responsibility for their disobedience. The wonder is that the disavowals of primal and other sorts of religious guilt took so long to develop. One might have expected them sooner.

To put this more finely: psychological explanations of primal guilt are not really rebellions against it. They are not even rejections of it. They are simply alternative methods of accounting for a widespread if not universal guilty condition that is often regarded as inherent. As such, they constitute renewed acceptances of it, as though such guilt had taken out a fresh lease on life by assuming a secular instead of a religious or spiritual existence. The guilt of the obsessive neurotic may actually be the divine Mata Hari of modern life, the priestly spy in the agnostic's and atheist's bedroom.

The unconscious, moreover, whether collective in the Jungian sense or not, may be a less exciting instrument of human mental activity than is usually assumed. It may process bizarre and important material, but it manages to do so in a completely neutral way. Whether, as in dreams, it does so sensibly, according to some sort of language, is a moot point. It may simply be making a mess of the images that it invents and marshals in its little, sometimes frightening dream stories. Its vaunted language may only be a language in retrospect, in which the mess is equipped with a false coherence by conscious observers. One of the most obvious if misused abilities of the human mind, after all, is to establish connections between any things at all, including a great many that certainly have nothing to do with each other. In the light of this possibility, the unconscious may simply be a type of mental civil servant, eternally sorting and stamping unrelated image-documents, which it fails to comment on, analyse or evaluate. Quite idly, it assumes no responsibility for what it does. The conscious mind, by contrast, thus bears the burden of the guilty indifference and everlasting smugness of the unconscious. If the unconscious may have neither courage nor cleverness, the conscious mind seldom takes a holiday. Its business will be to make plausible connections and choices, often ethical ones, and often to make a fool of itself as it does so.

The true rebels against the very idea of guilt – not criminal guilt, but the automatic emotional and religious varieties – are Schopenhauer, who is too pessimistic to see any sense in it; Nietzsche, who is too exuberant to see it as more than a pernicious fiction; Byron, who finds it vulgar; and Shelley, who considers it a loathsome political manipulation. There are others – Strindberg, for example, who laughs at it as at a puerile joke that no adult could be expected to take seriously; and Walt Whitman, whose happy mysticism renders questions of a guilty relation to God inane – but these four are the most influential.

Arthur Schopenhauer (1788-1860), though not melancholy himself, produced a philosophy so depressing as to cause its dismissal by many rival philosophers. Nonetheless, he remains one of the most dazzling of German stylists. While not normally as bellicose as Beethoven, who liked to throw eggs at waiters, he once heaved a woman who annoyed him down a flight of stairs. He felt no guilt at causing her injury, and when she died a number of years later, after he had regularly paid her a court-ordered compensation, he noted in his diary, 'Woman dead, debt concluded.'

This is not the place to consider his running skirmishes with Hegel, who struck him as an oaf, or with Hegel's followers, whom he regarded as dunces, or even his philosophical departures from Kant, which led to his belief that things in themselves (*Dinge an sich*, in Kant's famous phrase) could in fact be known (where

Kant had declared that this was impossible), but only through an inner examination of one's private acts of will. What is important to an examination of rebellions against guilt is Schopenhauer's conviction that history, including the history of the universe, has no meaning. It consists simply in the working out of a blind will. This will is not rational in any ordinary way; nor is it possessed of ideals, grace, consciousness, imagination and selfconsciousness. As Schopenhauer describes it in *The World as Will and Representation* (1818), the will of everything simply thrusts into being forces and creatures packed with its own competitiveness, ferocity, coldness, insensitivity and random dissolution, as well as powers of regeneration. The purest of accidents has led to the emergence of human beings capable of self-reflection, and of contemplating the existence of this will in themselves and everything else.

Because the existence of primal guilt implies that the universe itself is an ethical process, Schopenhauer's denial of the ethics of the will governing everything constitutes a complete rejection of meaningful, ultimate guilt. If this will is a-moral, the passages in Genesis describing Creation as an ethical act, a good one, are likewise meaningless: 'And God said, Let there be light: and there was light. And God saw the light, that it was *good* [italics inserted].' From the point of view of pure will, there can be nothing either good or bad about light. Nothing is any more important than anything else. There is no moral basis to reality. The assumption that it has a moral foundation is the result of human beings confusing themselves with cosmic events, or of anthropomorphism. This is not the result of an illness in the psychological sense: it is merely a mistake. Criminal law, too, has no intrinsic relationship to some type of natural ethics, or what has been termed Natural Law. It is not inherently better to preserve life than to destroy it: this is only better from the viewpoint of most human beings, who identify their own existence with life.

Schopenhauer was heavily influenced by the *Upanishads* and other Hindu Vedic texts, as was his contemporary, the American poet-philosopher Ralph Waldo Emerson (1803-82); but where Emerson was led into ethical forms of Transcendental mysticism,

Schopenhauer disparaged any sort of mysticism as rubbish. In taking so extreme a position, he rejected the ethical and theistic centres of Hinduism as well. At the bottom of reality, he maintained, there is only '*nichts*', or 'nothing', which is often mistranslated as 'nothingness' by philosophers and critics unwilling to accept his radicalism because they find it too drastic. 'Nothingness', it is worth remarking, has no discernible meaning, but it sounds pleasanter. In fact, there is no avoiding Schopenhauer's iron pessimism, beside which the doctrine of Original Sin looks like a disguised boon. The only balms offered to suffering humanity by his outlook are selfconscious meditation on humanity's lost condition, and art, whose beauty can lift the mind above a strangling reality. Even these provide only a momentary and insalubrious relief.

Schopenhauer's emphasis on irrationality, or meaninglessness, along with will, later acts as an initial stimulus to Freudian thinking about instinct and the role of the unconscious. His impact is also to be seen in the incandescent gloom of Joseph Conrad's *Heart of Darkness*, in which the European anti-hero Kurtz discovers what he believes to be 'the horror' of the moral aridity of the universe in the Belgian Congo and in his own soul. An equally dynamic impact of Schopenhauer's thought may be seen in such major works as *Thus Spake Zarathustra* (1883-85), *Beyond Good and Evil* (1885-86) and *The Genealogy of Morals* (1887) of Friedrich Nietzsche (1844-1900).

It may still be too late to rescue Nietzsche from his atrocious exploitation by the Nazis. Eventually, one assumes, the clock will be set back to allow for his heady originality. To suggest that his idea of the *Übermensch*, or overman, has nothing in common with cartoonish Nazi warrior types, and everything to do with emotional and spiritual enlightenment, remains a delicate matter among those who recall how well his apparent paeans to war were made to serve genocidal purposes. It is true that Nietzsche wrote for shock effect. His prose is a witty furnace. In it, he forges high, snowy peaks, between which spread no reasonable, connecting valleys, as he himself describes this unusual technique. He expects his readers to leap from one peak to the next through the champagne air, which he also supplies, inventing their own imaginative methods for doing so, and regardless of how free-associative these might be. One result of Nietzsche's quasi-biblical style is that while his aphorisms often prove shocking enough, they also and easily attract the attention of the unscrupulous and wicked.

His intention is to *épater* the 'afterworldly', as his prophet-hero Zarathustra labels all those Christians and others who have willingly enslaved themselves to ancient religious visions of heaven and hell. These concepts are worse than absurd, because they seduce their adherents into sacrificing their lives in this world for the sake of a non-existent next world. Good and evil, in their theological senses, are two more such mephitic notions. Original Sin, or primal guilt of whatever sort, is another. The struggles of Dostoyevski's Stavrogin would thus seem clownish to Nietzsche's Zarathustra, whose enlightened release from Church-manufactured unworthiness leads only to joy. Georg, in Kafka's 'The Judgement', would also no doubt strike Zarathustra as a pathetic example of someone who has foolishly sold his future to a fictional paternal divinity. Zarathustra knows no such conflicts as Georg's, but then he has chosen to live in a cave, far away from everyone. The only menace that he fears is that he might, in a moment of inexcusable weakness, take pity on those who do not share his enlightened condition. Pity might lure him into returning to human society, which would cause the ruination of his enlightenment. Pity must therefore be rejected.

On the surface, Nietzsche's acid attacks on institutional and mental slavery, or institution guilt, or even nation guilt – 'To be a good German, you must de-germanize yourself' – resemble those of William Blake (1757-1827) in his 'Proverbs of Hell': 'Sooner murder an infant in its cradle than nurse unacted desires'; 'Drive your cart and your plough over the bones of the dead'; 'Prisons are built with stones of Law, Brothels with bricks of Religion.' Blake's assaults, however, are directed at religious hypocrisy and corrupt political institutions, and in no sense at Christianity or the idea of Original Sin. It is curious that Blake is termed a Romantic. While he clearly yearns for a social and religious washing up so as to create a purified 'New Albion' in England, his temperament is essentially that of a religious conservative, or even reactionary, at least by eighteenth-century Rationalist standards. He might have felt most at home among flocks of moralizing biblical prophets. The atmosphere of his poetry is that of a celestial yet oblique antiquity rather than modernity. It is deeply anti-scientific. It thus lies well apart not only from Nietzsche but from the modern rebelliousness of George Gordon, Lord Byron (1788-1824).

Byron's frisky modernity emerges not simply in his rejection of all guilty relations to God, and nearly all other forms of guilt besides, but also in his promotion of himself as the first Byronic hero. This defiant figure is desolate, flippant, adventurous and maniacally haunted. He manages, at least in his impressions made on readers, always to be located atop a craggy height in the midst of a violent thunderstorm. This bad weather is part of his stage equipment and should alarm no one. Neither should his saturnine pose. In life, Byron was resourceful, practical, principled and rich. He was an ironic, astute and pugnacious self-publicist. Still, it is part of the self-abusive destiny of the Byronic hero that he take himself too seriously at the wrong moments, perhaps to confuse his detractors. In Byron's case, this led to his untimely, ghastly death of malaria, contracted while participating in the Greek war of independence of 1823.

Byron remains a Christian while obviously feeling uncomfortable with traditional tenets of Christianity, such as intrinsic guilt and Original Sin. These appear demeaning, or even in poor taste, especially in the face of the ennobling, harmonious forces of nature. He accepts and rebels simultaneously. He amazes with his frank acknowledgement of personal conflict, where lesser poets quickly have their minds made up. His poetry, which reveals a descriptive and technical mastery unrivalled in English, and matched only by Dante and Goethe in other languages, wrestles with the ravages of Time. Time, which demolished Rome, is the destroyer of human greatness, yet the sanctifier of artistic success. Prometheus, whom he views as the quintessential artist, as does Shelley, because he stole fire from the gods, committed the crime of being 'kind', and rendering 'less/The sum of human wretchedness'. His spirit is 'Triumphant where it dares defy' ('Prometheus'). In *Don Juan* and *Childe Harold's Pilgrim-*

age, which set the stamp of Byron's complex personality on Romanticism, the poet who has 'seen the sick and ghastly bed/Of Sin delirious with its dread' ('The Prisoner of Chillon'), forces himself to 'ponder boldly' that 'the beam' of heaven and 'the truth' nonetheless 'pours in' on the 'unprepared mind' despite the 'false nature' of human life with its 'uneradicable taint of sin':

> Our life is a false nature – 'tis not in
> The harmony of things, – this hard decree,
> This uneradicable taint of sin,
> This boundless upas, this all-blasting tree,
> Whose root is earth, whose leaves and branches be
> The skies which rain their plagues on men like dew –
> Disease, death, bondage – all the woes we see –
> And worse, the woes we see not – which throb through
> The immedicable soul, with heart-aches ever new.
>
> Yet let us ponder boldly – 'tis a base
> Abandonment of reason to resign
> Our right of thought – our last and only place
> Of refuge; this, at least, shall still be mine:
> Though from our birth the faculty divine
> Is chan'd and tortured – cabin'd, cribb'd, confined,
> And bred in darkness, lest the truth should shine
> Too brightly on the unprepared mind,
> The beam pours in, for time and skill will couch the blind.
> (*Childe Harold's Pilgrimage*, Canto IV)

The beam, which seems strangely more available to the poet than anyone else, and which may be powerful enough to stimulate political as well as religious freedom, upsets the applecart of any traditional ideas of guilt.

The applecart is not merely upset but smashed to pieces, or that at least was the intent, by Percy Bysshe Shelley (1792-1822). Shelley had been sent down from Oxford in 1811 for publishing a pamphlet, *The Necessity of Atheism*, which questioned the authority of Christianity more than denied it, but he thereafter denied it with increasing ease, especially with respect to the

Church's doctrine of Original Sin and other notions of religious guilt.

These he more and more came to see as political weapons whose purpose was to plunder democracy, subdue populations and steam-engine ghastly European tyrannies. 'Christless, Godless' England was ruled by 'An old, mad, blind, despised and dying king', stupid princes, 'Golden and sanguine laws which tempt and slay' and a spirit-draining narcosis of religious exploitation ('Sonnet: England in 1819'). In 'The Sensitive Plant' he painted an Eden in which Eve dies alone and unsinning, the garden rots after her death, poisonous weeds take over and paradise itself is exposed as a neo-Platonic mocking dream. He celebrated passive resistance to political suppression in 'The Mask of Anarchy', and peaceful revolutions to establish democracy, which he defined as 'the equilibrium between institutions and opinions', in 'Ode to Naples' and 'Ode to Liberty'. A constant theme is that 'Religion veils her eyes' to autocratic viciousness and that a true apprehension of the divine has been captivated by the superstitious wizardry of 'The Galilean serpent' which left the 'world an undistinguishable heap' ('Ode to Liberty'). These are intensely modern ideas, but it is crucial to note that their strength derives from their extraordinary expression, or from Shelley's literary genius. His muscular, sweet lines constantly show the full range of the possibilities of guilt, and freedom from it, even while attacking it, in phrases that seem either unruly nights when the burly wind bashes at the panes and sniggers and barks in the chimney, or lashed with the reflected, serene glimmers of crystalline if thunderous mountain cataracts. Even after Shelley comes to believe not in any god of religion but in 'the awful shadow of some unseen Power/[that] Floats though unseen among us', and which is 'Dear, and yet dearer for its mystery' ('Hymn to Intellectual Beauty'), he remains pre-eminently the artist rather than the propagandist, aware of the subtle paradoxes, galling contradictions and infinite ironies of his fellow human beings. Mere ideology constantly surrenders to the greater complexities of perfecting his style and music.

Nowhere is Shelley's portrait of the oppressiveness of religious guilt more sharply drawn than in his drama *Prometheus Un-*

bound. The heroic thief of the divine fire, who is punished for
three thousand years by Jupiter, 'the tyrant of the world', has torn
'the painted veil' from life and offered humanity pure freedom:

> The loathsome mask has fallen, the man remains
> Sceptreless, free, uncircumscribed, but man
> Equal, unclassed, tribeless, and nationless,
> Exempt from awe, worship, king, degree, the king
> Over himself; just, gentle, wise: but man
> Passionless? – no, yet free from guilt or pain,
> Which were, for his will made or suffered them,
> Nor yet exempt, though ruling them like slaves,
> From chance, and death, and mutability,
> The clogs of that which else might oversoar
> The loftiest star of unascended heaven,
> Pinnacled dim in the intense inane.
>
> (IV, iii, 193-204)

The grandeur of Shelley's conception of human freedom here
springs, as elsewhere in his poetry, from its Idealism, which is
derived from Plato, and its defect from its failure to acknowledge
that many people, like tyrannical gods, might enjoy both evil and
guilt and have no desire to be rid of them. A problem with such
Idealistic thinking generally lies in its assumption that all human beings are alike in motives. These are presumed to be as
good, as virtuous, as the Idealist's own. Amidst a gathering and
pure utopianism, little thought is given to the existence of the
macabre delights of horrid pleasures, or to the masses of people
who have cultivated them, willingly sacrificing happiness to
bestial ecstasies, and who continue to cultivate them. The delec-
tations of Satan are certainly neither abstractions nor fantasies,
no matter how abominable or destructive they may also be.
Schopenhauer, for all the dourness of his outlook, had arrived at
a similarly innocent utopian prescription: a minimal exercise of
human wilfulness must produce a steep decline in human suffering and guilt. No doubt this is true, but it fails to take account of
human diversity, or even of the occasionally cruel whims of the
saints among us.

2. Hamlet and the New Injustice

The model, though not the source, of all these and many other modern rebellions against guilt, at least in recent centuries, is Hamlet. Oscar Wilde once remarked that before Shakespeare created this strange, fascinating and guilt-obsessed figure there was no such person, and that afterwards there were thousands. Sometimes Hamlet is a negative model, as in T.S. Eliot's 'The Love Song of J. Alfred Prufrock' (1917), in which the self-denying and guilt-swathed protagonist, who is as punctilious a failure as Kafka's Georg, fingers himself: 'No! I am not Prince Hamlet, nor was meant to be;/ Am an attendant lord, one that will do/ To swell a progress, start a scene or two,/ Advise the Prince; no doubt an easy tool,/ Deferential, glad to be of use,/ Politic, cautious and meticulous': a Hamlet bundled into a Polonius, for whom the higher, spiritual forms of guilt have become obsolete, yet conscious of Shakespeare's Danish prince as the model for incomprehensible guilt and for flurried refutations of it.

On rare occasions, the Shakespearian influence is merely side-stepped – in Walt Whitman's mystical apprehension of the universe as glorious harmony, for instance, which corks up all the old valves of guilty affection and guilty pain, and banishes several thousand years of the commanding guilty genius, all the swart, fearful strictures, in lines whose blitheness must seem to many no more than a lovely cheat:

> The myth of heaven indicates the soul,
> The soul is always beautiful, it appears more or it
>   appears less, it comes or it lags behind,
> It comes from its embower'd garden and looks pleasantly
>   on itself and encloses the world,
> Perfect and clean the genitals previously jetting, and
>   perfect and clean the womb cohering,
> The head well-grown proportion'd and plumb, and the
>   bowels and joints proportion'd and plumb.
>
>   ('The Sleepers', 7; 1855)

Whitman's endlessly aureoled stanzas, one cannot help but notice, permeated as in these lines with his boundless optimism, or even elsewhere when they praise democracy and laud ordinary people – carpenters, mothers, fishermen, children, farmers and young women – are curiously devoid of individuals who experience conflict. He depicts generalized people, as do many Idealists, among them Blake and often Shelley – rather than the inwardly tormented. It is these that matter in rebellions against guilt.

What these people know, and what Hamlet knows, is that their major problem is that opportunity, plus conflict and choice, almost inevitably lead into remorse. Often remorse leads further, into some sort of punishing guilt, either for the road not taken or the road taken. It is not necessary to take a fearful glimpse into the dark well of sociopathology, with its diseased and irresponsible, its unethical abolition of all guilty feelings, or the darker well of conscious, outright evil, the evil often freely chosen by healthy minds, to understand this common condition of human conflict, or torment. Guilt always gains as easy an entrance into the human psyche as evil or appetites, or for many, goodness.

This fearful difficulty may be put more simply. Either we do or do not have free will. If we do have it, and if we allow for the varying circumstances in which we may exercise varying amounts of it, we have no choice but to accept that we must pay for it. What it costs is usually guilt, and the price is inevitably outrageous, filthy, suppurating, unfunny, savaging – and worth it. In the midst of paying for it, anyone is often hard put to sustain a decent sense of humour, though a grotesque sense of irony, and even a fetid love of the grotesque, or on occasion a splendid creative energy, may explode in anyone's guilty breast. One's good cheer may wither. It may improve. The time must seem out of joint. The expense of spirit in a waste of shame will seem as nothing compared to the price of sorrow paid by the soul that is left parched by guilt.

Hamlet remains the most translucent prism of this grieving, illuminating terror of the modern soul. He is historically located on the cusp between medieval Augustinian guilt and Reformation reactions to it. From the viewpoint of the history of guilt and the Reformation's and subsequent social earthquakes in progress when it was written (1601), Shakespeare's play thus looms as momentous.

Hamlet's entire struggle is with guilt: to expunge it, to banish it, to redeem his closeted guilty kingdom in which everyone is somehow guilty of one thing or another, or will shortly be. His own guilt, and that of Denmark in the play, are, on the one hand, old – incestuous, like Oedipus', or usurping, like Satan's and the guilt of Adam and Eve; and, on the other hand, new – abased and hesitant, or devoted to horrid guilt itself, in the ways of Kafka's Georg and Dostoyevski's Stavrogin. Hamlet tries to shrug off these possibilities of guilt – he is in many ways a modern man – by simply rejecting them, and finds that he cannot: his royal culpability can only be intensified if he does nothing to avenge the apparent murder of his father.

In a real sense, his problem is that he is born too early, before the Middle Ages and Renaissance have relaxed their grip on popular beliefs in ghosts. As a result, he is left in the quandary of having to do nothing until he can actually confirm the murder – and only then, perhaps, of administering justice by killing his uncle and now-king, Claudius, himself the guilty regicide. By nature, in other words, Hamlet is neither hesitant nor indecisive. He is supremely ethical in a modern lawyer's way, but at the wrong time. He might easily agree with Justice William Blackstone's eighteenth-century precept that 'it is better that ten guilty persons escape than one innocent suffer'. Hamlet is determined to do the right legal thing, and it is precisely his comprehension of a new legal ethics, in the face of shifting cultural ideas about guilt, of what constitutes evidence of criminal wrongdoing, that produces his hesitation and indecision. Information gleaned from a ghost is plainly insufficient, and especially not from a ghost that itself starts 'like a guilty thing upon a fearful summons'. He must 'have grounds more relative than this'. Can he find them?

It would be a mistake to dismiss this ghost business too easily, or to treat it too lightly. Guilt has traditionally been seen as no more puissant than ghosts. In Shakespeare's day the belief in ghosts, while increasingly mocked, was widely accepted. As late as the eighteenth century, respected scientists were still investigating ghosts (no doubt the belief in them continues into the present day, but it is the scientific propriety that is here at issue). Researchers devoted peculiar careers to describing their habits and qualities. An ancient superstition held that the guilt of murderers activated ghosts, propelling them hither and yon, but as Johann Heinrich Jung (1740-1817) pointed out in his block-head book, *Theory of Ghosts*, while the spirits of the departed can cavort about, stand on their heads and change their complexions, they cannot move anything at all, not even a grain of sand. Jung-Stilling, as he was known, spent years looking into this matter, and probably knew as much about it as anyone is likely to learn. Thus the ghost of Hamlet's father, who rushes away at cockcrow on his 'fearful summons', needs Hamlet to execute his vengeance on Claudius. Alone, he can do nothing, or almost nothing, for he can in fact speak, doing so at almost interminable length.

It is revealing, this ability of ghosts to speak, or at least to communicate. It suggests salient features not of ghosts but of the guilt with which they have to do. What is important, surely, is that guilt itself is deeply connected to loquacity, or to a dread of it. 'Murder will out' echoes not merely a tenacious and old conviction, but also a fact about guilt, that it seems virtually to compel speech (in contrast to embarrassment, remorse, shame and responsibility, which have no such associations). At the same time, guilt has always been linked to prayer. The idea of the modern autobiography is traceable into ancient Jewish notions of atonement, St Augustine's *Confessions* and the pious Christian confessional itself. Hovering behind any modern autobiography, even one as witty as Mark Twain's or Benjamin Franklin's, is a smidgeon of personal guilt and a quest of expiation, albeit recreated as jesting and candied laughter. Any guilty passion, which is by definition cut off from the offended cosmos, seems to ache for curative prayer, and for reconciliation with nature and the divine. Claudius himself prays for this – his guilt seeks consoling expression – yet in refusing to give up his throne and queen, or the profits of his crime, his vacuous words 'fly up' while his thoughts 'remain below'. His prayers are useless.

It is in this psychologically plausible context of the need of guilt to find release, to discover the appropriate language that will reconnect the guilty murderer to the universe at large and to the divine, that Hamlet searches for convincing evidence of Claudius' murder of his father. He finds it, also revealingly, by arranging a performance of a play, the play-within-the-play, 'The Mousetrap'. He knows that 'Foul deeds will rise,/Though all the earth o'erwhelm them, to men's eyes', and has heard

> That guilty creatures sitting at a play
> Have, by the very cunning of the scene,
> Been struck so to the soul that presently
> They have proclaim'd their malefactions.
> For murder, though it have no tongue, will speak
> With most miraculous organ.
>
> (II, ii, 584-9)

The 'miraculous organ' is merely the God-prompted power of speech of the guilt-rattled murderer. A bit of a jab is what is necessary to puncture the feeble membrane of the killer's restraint. At that point, Hamlet reasons, the horrid, explosive energy must out. The murderer will helplessly exchange the risk of capture and even punishment for the relief of its release. Healing will matter more to him than freedom.

To this, though, it must be added that, as Hamlet well knows, Claudius is no Iago. Unlike the hell-ensconced arch-fiend, of whom Iago is an incarnation (and in fact a well-known extension of the Vice figure of medieval mystery plays), who delights in evil for its own sake and who feels neither guilt nor torment for his crimes, Claudius is thoroughly human, easily tempted and deeply old-fashioned. He is in fact the shocking type of a ferocious, cunning Prufrock, but a Prufrock without inhibitions, who hates himself for his own weakness and who as a consequence loves power. It is precisely Claudius' inner – or as Jung might argue, his individuated – conflicts that produce his unbearable guilt and compel its release.

Hamlet itself, therefore, presents a world of familiar, ghost-certified guilt, in which the hero rebels against the very idea of this sort of thing. The hero uses another play to check on the truth, and the two plays together equal a slap-up of crossed lightning bolts, of worlds in collision.

There is more to all this. How religious is Hamlet, and in what ways? That he subscribes to some extent to traditional Christian beliefs is shown by his refusal to kill Claudius while he is praying, because the guilty king – and by this point, after the performance of the play-within-the-play, Hamlet knows that he is guilty – may then, according to common ideas about those who try to purge their souls through prayer, simply be dispatched to heaven when he ought be sent to hell. Hamlet also believes in the biblical notion that any man who commits adultery with his brother's wife (and the wife herself, his mother) is guilty of incest. Beyond this, however, the question of Hamlet's religious beliefs becomes opaque. What is illuminating is his statement to his close friend, Horatio: 'There are more things in heaven and earth, Horatio,/Than are dreamt of in your philosophy.'

What are these things? The most interesting, though it has developed for several centuries by the time Hamlet comes to consider his horrific problem, is a cultural tacking away, straight across the Western world, from deductive to inductive thinking. Induction, or taking on the evidence of a belief before accepting it as true, or at least seeking a solid mix of evidence and hypothetical deduction, was becoming increasingly fashionable by Shakespeare's day. This shift had already provoked a major intellectual and social rebellion, in which masses of people had objected to the Church's denial of the validity of sense data and sensual experience, and in which they had dismissed the old clerical suspicions of the five senses and of what they demonstrate about physical reality.

Shakespeare's play makes a direct connection to this great change. The tormented hero is a student at Wittenberg, one of the centres of the new, inductive physical sciences, a university, in other words, that is a defender of the still-controversial heliocentric system of Copernicus (1473-1543). Shakespeare himself, as the research of Peter Usher has shown, knew the English scientist Thomas Digges, whose *Perfit Description* (1576) itself supported the Copernican description of the universe against the millennium-old Ptolemaic system of nine spheres. Hamlet, therefore, must be seen as one of the most modern, adventurous, inductive thinkers, and as fascinated by the new astronomy. At a minimum, he seems unconvinced by theology and any of the old explanations, including those having to do with any of the old ways of guilt.

In his very ingenuity, however, and in his imaginative modernity, lies the source of his bitter death. Classical tragedy more or less stipulates two conditions (though they are not mentioned by Aristotle), among a host of lesser ones, which virtually guarantee the terrible, ironic outcome: that the hero possesses a profound sensitivity to guilt, and that he (or she) entertains a religious or cosmic scepticism. Oedipus, to cite this fabulous paradigm once more, though deeply ethical, and alert to the chances of his own future guilt, is dubious of the powers of the gods to govern his fate. His ridiculous but understandable hubris convinces him that he can defy their prophecies, though to everyone else this idea seems absurd.

Hamlet shares both Oedipus' gnawing alertness to guilt and his scepticism about established cosmic explanations, with the latter on an even grander scale, though not his hubris. The result is that Shakespeare's eccentric, clever hero, who is notorious for his procrastination as he seeks vengeance for his father's murder, is transfixed, or as it were, hypnotized, by questions about the meaning of guilt in the totally new universe in which he sees himself as living. This fact cannot but betray him, though, as the cogs and winches of the fierce old world – the ruthless choices of old-fashioned others, especially Claudius – drag him, even as he hesitates, toward Laertes' 'anointed' sword and his infelicitous, cathartic death.

In considering the issue of guilt in Hamlet's world, moreover, and of Hamlet himself as the most influential model for guilt's later history, what is significant is that the play allows for no usual or traditional justice. He who looks for it, despite his new ideas about the cosmos, is himself doomed, probably as a result of the act of looking for it, and with his death everyone's purposes are shown to be 'mistook', and quickly fall 'on th'inventors' heads'.

A comparison, again, with Sophocles' *Oedipus*, from this point of view, or even with others of Shakespeare's tragedies, excepting perhaps *King Lear*, could not be more revealing. In *Oedipus*, as the hero-investigator of the terrible crimes of king-murder and incest discovers that he himself is the criminal whom he is hunting, and is punished, it becomes obvious that he deserves his punishment. Hamlet does not. From any reasonable standpoint, Hamlet is innocent. He represents the power of justice in his world, and he is murdered. It scarcely matters, as one realizes this, that a type of capital justice is actually administered to Claudius and Gertrude, the murderous king and queen. Justice in *Hamlet* seems to amount to little more than primitive retribution. It appears gratuitous. The audience, which at least on a subliminal level is aware of these facts, cannot but intuit a frightening additional fact: that with *Hamlet* the world itself has entered a novel, nervous, unchristian era, in which common justice has become as elusive as God, and in which a corrosive, unredeemable guilt seems to spread indiscriminately in all directions.

Neither does the play offer any hint that much of this spreading guilt is itself traditional. Certainly it is not simply the guilt of Original Sin, or 'Man's first disobedience'. It possesses a strange impersonality. It hums horribly beneath the Danish court's palatial surfaces. It seems to stretch straight across Hamlet's star-darkened universe – as if the universe itself had suddenly been reborn in darkness, or as if it were suddenly exposed as very old, and absolutely, prodigiously unknown to everybody, and especially to the old religions of Judaism and Christianity, whose influence is loosening as it makes clear its alien presence.

IV

The Source of Modern Guilt

1. Desire, Infinity and Guilt

To understand it thoroughly, and to see its source, we need to change the dimensions of the discussion. We need to look afresh at modern times and history, taking note of several events which have not so far been considered in tandem.

It is easiest to begin with a startling though obvious fact: the only genuine human problem is the problem of desire. All other problems, and these in no mean or superficial way, are bound to it by steely or silken ligatures. All religions, in their moral and even spiritual aspects, confront the issue of desire, seeking to temper it, channel it, dam it and often condemn it. Distortions of desire form nearly the whole of the subject matter of the world's literature. They are the chief exercising levers of the world's legal systems. Desire is the source of inner conflict. Desire is the source of peace, as well as love, sex, murder, joy and the human achievements that matter to everyone, along with those that are secret or failures and matter to no one. In its modern peregrinations, a worship of an unusual form of desire is in fact the source of modern guilt.

To be clear, desire is never merely appetite. An amoeba has appetites. It is absurd to speak of an amoeba as having desires. At the other end of the animate scale, it feels peculiar to speak of whales, despite fashionable modern hopes to the contrary, as passionate. So far as one can tell, whales lack desires, though they exhibit loyalties and appetites which in comparison to human ones are enormous and even incomprehensible. The difference between desire and appetite can be located in the human faculty of imagination, which may also be described as the abstract languages of fantasy, dreaming, anticipating, wishing and visualizing. Amoebas cannot imagine anything. Neither, apparently, can whales. While dogs dream, and exhibit yearnings to the extent that their domestication has led them into loyalties of a deep-felt sort, any description of their psyches as containing desires is not only questionable but hardly worth pausing over except among fanatical dog-fanciers. Most people would probably not accept the proposition that the loyalties and hostilities of dogs, or other species of animals, in serious ways approximate the complicated and often uncontrollable devotions and ambitions of their human friends and enemies. Fido is not Hamlet, nor can pretend to be. Fido is also not Laertes, or the psychological equivalent of the most imbecile servant or nobleman at the court of the prissiest king in any of Shakespeare's plays, or in history itself. The quality of imagination is absent. Canine dreams lack imaginative creativity.

Even the cloudy question of suicide sinks beneath the larger and cloudier question of desire itself, encoffined perhaps in one of its cellars, or dormant in one of its suburbs. Camus was in error when he described suicide as the only philosophical problem, in *Le Mythe de Sisyphe* (1942). Suicide itself results from frustrated ambitions, from crippled and stormy desires. Nor for many can death, even suicidal death, be seen as the end of desire. In Dante's forest of suicides, in his *Inferno* (c. 1300-21), a horrible torment continues after death for the ghosts of the self-slaughterous. In a number of religious and philosophical systems, such as those of the Hindus and Pythagoreans, reincarnation ultimately prevents the act of suicide from solving any but immediate problems.

Nor is the possible meaninglessness of one's life, or life itself, affected in the slightest by one's decision to remove oneself from it. Lives achieve their meanings, or lose them, through the vital acts of the lively. Any act of suicide, if committed, neither adds to nor detracts from the meaningfulness of the life that is cut short. The barbarity of Nero's life, his willingness to engage in mass murder, is not altered because he killed himself. Othello's calm self-cancellation with a dagger is an honourable gesture consistent with an honourable life, albeit one driven at the end by dishonourable, guilty desires. Othello's suicide, however, does not create the meaning of this life. Only his life creates it. His life keeps creating it. Othello is a dramatic incarnation. He can be made to recreate his life and suicide constantly, each time with a different import for audiences that view the question of his suicide differently, as often callously as with commiseration.

To most people it is perhaps obvious that the act of suicide is without philosophical or ontological significance, though it may for some serve a practical purpose. The moon will still shine on the wet streets of the world, bringing its puddled reflection. The loon will still seem to mourn. Hope will die. It will flare. Desire – the exquisite aching, the fiery quest – will remain its glorious and imaginative source. Suicide is the rejection of desire. It is the final rejection of imagination. The poet W.H. Auden (1907-73) once remarked stoically that he had never for an instant considered suicide. While hard to believe, his remark indicates the limitations of his often splendid poetry. What it means is that he could not conceive, in a sympathetic way, of the rejection of imagination, that he could not contemplate an end to meaning. He could not, in other words, have written *Othello*.

In any materialistic society, materialistic desires rapidly come to assume an exaggerated importance. This is probably self-evident. What is perhaps not so obvious is that in any such society desire itself must soon assume this type of strange importance, that spiritual desires too may now become exaggerations, paralysing in their sheer hugeness. They may indeed become too large for the universe itself, turning into stupendous annihilations. While this condition, or possibility, is traceable to some extent into nearly every human culture, and is as typical of the hedonism of the decadent Rome of Petronius as it is of the pathetic spiritual Flagellants of the High Middle Ages, it has only recently, in the past two hundred years, become a powerful, dominant fashion in modern Western cultures. It is precisely this new Western (and spreading) exhibitionism of desire, in which it comes to lack anchors in values, in which it becomes a force too great for the human heart to bear, and for the human mind to grasp, that is the new human condition. It is also the root of the new, tormenting features of modern guilt.

To avoid any confusion on this point, one must quickly add that this sort of desire is only rarely viewed as an obsession, or as some glamorous enchantment of possessed, hysterical, hallucinatory, rash and greedy people. On the contrary, it is almost invariably understood as a form of health. It is puffed as the sober and even ideal destiny of all human beings.

The French poet Charles Baudelaire is among the first to present it in this way, with terrifying audacity, in 1857:

> Pour l'enfant, amoureaux de cartes et d'estampes,
> L'universe est égal à son vaste appetit.
> Ah, que le monde est grand à la clarté des lampes!
> Aux yeux du souvenir que le monde est petit!
>
> Un matin nous partons, le cerveau plein de flamme,
> Le coeur gros de rancune et de désirs amers,
> Et nous allons, suivant le rythme de la lame,
> Berçant notre infini sur le fini des mers.
>
> ('Le Voyage')
>
> [For children, mad for maps and foreign stamps,
> The universe seems a match for their appetite.
> How huge the earth seems, lit by study lamps!
> How minuscule in memory's dimming sight!
>
> One morning we set sail, brains full of fire,
> Our heart's desire a rank acerbity,
> And seek to soothe, with rhythms of the oar,
> Our boundlessness upon the finite sea.]

What is revealing here is the process by which a boundless childhood appetite develops into the seductive tyranny of an equally boundless adult desire – and the fate of this desire. The eager children of the first stanza, in other words, peering by lamplight at their colourful maps and foreign stamps, turn naturally bold and adventurous. Their appetite becomes as big as the universe. Even the earth at this point seems huge to them.

What follows, however, in the second stanza and others after it, is a peculiar and strained sense of betrayal, which in no way reflects their having merely grown up and met with disappointments. Now fully adult and capable, these former children – we ourselves – feel 'rancune et de désirs amers', an unchecked bitterness, a conviction of blazing imprisonment. Only the sea's infinite rhythms can possibly salve and soothe, or douse, the infinite ferment of their misery. The grown-up children actually set sail, expecting finally to immerse their 'boundlessness' in the sea, and if possible to lose it there, but soon make the bitter discovery that the sea is finite. As the rest of the poem shows, this discovery is wickedly painful. An emotional entropy, an inner exhaustion of despair, dictated by their living idol of desire, whose powers continue to expand even as it experiences defeat, and which goes on ruling them even as they realize that they cannot exist without it, entices them into senseless further adventures, into a vacuous pursuit of the 'new' simply for its own sake, and at last into a guilty, meaningless quest of death. Only death, or even hell – but certainly not the earth, which they have now come to see as 'minuscule', and not the universe itself – may be vast enough to accommodate their (or our) desires.

Earlier in the century, in 1821, Shelley, in a letter describing the Protestant cemetery at Rome, evoked a similar capacity of human desires to expand infinitely. He also took stock of the new mission of these emotions, to populate a universe suddenly isolated and quite likely empty:

The English burying-place is a green slope near the walls, under the pyramidal tomb of Cestius, and is, I think, the most beautiful and solemn cemetery I ever beheld. To see the sun shining on its grass, fresh, when we first visited it, with the autumnal dews, and hear the whispering of the wind among the leaves of the trees which have overgrown the tomb of Cestius; and the soil which is stirring in the sun-warm earth, and to mark the tombs, mostly of women and young people who were buried there, one might, if one

were to die, desire the sleep they seem to sleep. Such is the
human mind, and so it peoples with its wishes vacancy and
oblivion.

In Shelley's lush clauses, desire is seen as a rescue from oblivion.
It is asked to people a peculiarly dull emptiness of time and
space, and to fill with its manufactured angels and scurvy demons a spiritual vacancy that lies beyond a physical barrenness.

What is pertinent to understanding modern guilt is that in
each of these passages by Baudelaire and Shelley the reader
encounters a simultaneously frightened and elated sense of infinite space-time. This, to be sure, is the fairly recently discovered
space-time of Copernicus' Renaissance universe, as revised by
Johannes Kepler (1571-1630), who showed that the planets
moved in ellipses rather than circles, and by Galileo Galilei
(1564-1642), who was the first to train a telescope on the moon,
discovering its mountains, and who made clear to everyone the
infinite reaches of outer space.

This new model of the universe is a mere two hundred years
old by the time Baudelaire and Shelley come to take stock of its
effects. It still awaits its mathematical description, in the twentieth century, by Albert Einstein (1879-1955), but is already
viewed by both poets as too large, bare and trivial to be
emotionally satisfying. It stimulates boundless desires, yet it
recompenses them only with a lax and smothering blank. The
result is that the desires themselves seem far more absorbing
than the infinite universe that induces them. As other nineteenth-century writers soon attest, the human imagination,
grown skittish in this tangled condition, may actually seek to
overwhelm space-time and physical reality altogether, by ignoring and exceeding them, belittling them with the grander
infinitude of desire itself, and with a form of desire that may
prove self-centering and abasing.

It is crucial to appreciate the bewitching novelty of Baudelaire's and Shelley's revelations. If the longing and rapid flogging
of this type of monumental desire seem somehow familiar to us,
they would hardly have seemed so to them or their contemporaries. The very idea of the opportunity that they describe, of

careening wildly into the infinite, was utterly unknown during the Middle Ages. Indeed, throughout medieval Europe, the concept of a mathematical infinity was unknown. (It had been discovered, with no use made of it, in the Indus Valley some five hundred years before the birth of Christ; it was rediscovered and introduced into the analytical geometry of Descartes, in the seventeenth century.)

Eternity, on the other hand, a rival concept to that of physical infinity, and one cherished throughout medieval Christendom, was taken to refer only to the mind of God. Eternity stood outside time, and was inscrutable and indescribable. It was not a fit subject for discussion, as St Augustine argues with science-crushing strictness in his *Enchiridion on Faith, Hope and Love*: 'It is not necessary to probe into the nature of things, as was done by those whom the Greeks call *physici*; nor need we be in alarm lest the Christian be ignorant of the elements – the motion, and order, and eclipses of the heavenly bodies; the form of the heavens; the species and nature of animals, plants, stones, fountains, rivers, mountains; about chronology and distances' (IX).

The medieval universe – unlike Baudelaire's and Shelley's infinite one – was not only finite but also a rounded, neat enclosure. It was encircled and embraced by heaven and the mind of God. The earth, a fixed orb, was located not so much at its centre as at its bottom. According to Augustine and other theologians, this was the single point in it farthest from primordial divine reality, the one spot most isolated from God's heavenly abode. (Here it must be added that the ambiguous meaning of the earth's location in the Ptolemaic System usually eludes modern historians of science and other writers, who continue to assert, merely on the basis of looking at mock-ups of the system, that medieval people thought of themselves as terribly important because they had been placed by God at the centre of the universe; actually, the reverse is the case, a fact that the contemporary literature indicates: people thought of themselves as 'wretched', using this term to describe their sense of divine desolation and indeed near, but by no means absolute, frightening abandonment by God.) Medieval ideas of religious guilt depended to a great extent on everyone's belief in the vast but finite and measurable distance that separated human beings from the celestial fires of God's heavenly 'Empyrean', or abode, past the outermost, or uppermost, of the Ptolemaic System's nine spheres.

Because of these medieval convictions, when one comes across infinite, idolized forms of desire in medieval literature, one finds that they are dismissed as lunacy. Frequently, they are the stuff of tragedy. Dante's capricious Ulysses, whose resemblance to Homer's Odysseus is slight, drives his ship and crew beyond the dun bourne of the known world. His irrepressible yearning for experiences beyond the human only flings him and his companions into a vicious whirlpool, and the eighth circle of Hell, that reserved for fraudulent counsellors. Richard III, in Shakespeare's Renaissance play, some centuries later, longs for the whole world 'to bustle in', and seldom has the verb 'bustle' exuded so rank and evil an odour. Crowded with assassinations, curses and fatuous bloody battles, Richard's tragic arena – Shakespeare himself called the play a tragedy – teems with the foul consequences of destructive, infinite desires. In Richard's ghastly death, it presents their, if not quite his, rebuke.

Marlowe's Doctor Faustus, another fatuous experimenter with the infinite, wishes to 'ransack the ocean for orient pearl'. He bargains with Mephistopheles for the chance to overthrow nature entirely: 'I'll be great emperor of the world,/ And make a bridge through the air/ To pass the ocean.' Thrust into Hell by demons at the expiration of his twenty-four-year pact with the devil, he nonetheless finds out that evil (at least in the popular thinking of his day) has its limits. Other specimen characters may be cited. The heroine of Webster's *The White Devil* (1611, or a full decade after *Hamlet*), Vittoria, speaks hopelessly, as she awaits her execution, of the possibilities of an infinity without God: 'My soul, like to a ship in a black storm,/Is driven, I know not whither.' The quasi-mystical desires of Gottfried von Strassburg's Tristan and Isolde (c. 1202), their devotion to an infinity of love, seek a transformation of their human longing for each other into a substitute for religion, recklessly rolling over the demands of society and the world. This goal rapidly produces a tragedy of poisonings and murders.

Even the satirical and serious political writing of the sixteenth century reflects a belief in finitude as health. Thomas More's *Utopia* (1516) paints a futuristic New World in which desire dies an unnaturally early death. For More, infinity exists only in his own boring ambition that the inhabitants of his earthly paradise wear an unending monotony of the same drab uniforms. Any other desire is mere profligacy.

One of the first to sound the new note is Sir Thomas Browne. In his *Hydriotaphia*, or *Urne-Buriall* (1658), he recommends an emotional and intellectual adventure that would have seemed imperilling, if not unhealthy, to artists, writers and nearly everyone else a mere sixty or so years earlier. In fact Browne is registering a new atmosphere. With the concept of infinity now in use in mathematics, Browne advocates what is to become the new human condition of infinite healthy desire, as he sees it, a condition that will be more acidly diagnosed by the poet Giacomo Leopardi in his *Fragment on Suicide* nearly two centuries later (1824). Browne exhorts his readers to partake of a delectable new joy:

> Let thy thoughts be of things which have not entered into the hearts of beasts: think of things long past, and long to come: acquaint thyself with the choragium of the stars, and consider the vast expanse beyond them. Let intellectual tubes give thee a glance of things which visive organs reach not. Have a glimpse of incomprehensibles; and thoughts of things, which thoughts but tenderly touch.

The door that leads not simply into another hidden chamber of the imagination, but out onto an interminable prairie of it, has been opened, and Browne's fertile 'intellectual tubes' will supply the rest. They will connect the mind's embryonic desires to the new infinity. These tubes are also the stalks of new hopes. That the hopes themselves are somehow also doomed things, breeders of novel and horrid frustrations, self-annihilations and eventually a new form of guilt, Browne does not, and perhaps could not, anticipate.

This is because the new and sweet-fragranced atmosphere,

spreading rapidly among the educated, seems to smother at first all suspicions of its more dangerous implications. Its sheer novelty seems a delicious relief. Desire and imagination seem about to create a new cosmic justice. Yet it is worth stressing that precisely the opposite of Browne's attitude toward unshackled imaginative passion, or infinite desire, appears in Thomas Nashe's *Pierce Penniless*, published sixty-four years earlier, in 1592.

Nashe is here out to defend the theatres of Shakespeare's day against those, the gathering Puritan many, who wished to close them down on grounds of immorality:

> In plays, all cozenages, all cunning drifts over-gilded with outward holiness, all stratagems of war, all the canker-worms that breed on the rust of peace, are most lively atomized. They shew the ill success of treason, the fall of hasty climbers, the wretched end of usurpers, the misery of civil dissension, and how God is ever more in punishing of murder.

The punishment that Nashe describes would have been perfectly intelligible to St Augustine: divine punishment could enthral sin. Nor is Browne's invitation to explore infinite imaginings in one-self and the universe everywhere accepted in his own day. The dissenters, for whom the giddy new atmosphere exercises little appeal, or none at all, are legion, and themselves influential. Spinoza (1632-77), Browne's exact contemporary, ranks first among them: 'The philosopher understands nature as a single substance equivalent to God, in which we all inhere as modes.' Spinoza's denial of an emotional infinity as acceptable, as in any way rational, because it is limited by the size of nature, which is the same as the size of God, is unique in its mixture of science with mysticism.

The new atmosphere, with its intrinsic threats to all rational ways of managing guilt, develops anyway. It becomes a fashion, evolving in quirky stages, often in coincidence with social changes. These changes gather like local and then allied storms. Combining in packs, they fall on older beliefs like felons. Like felons in fact, they unleash both perversity and nobility. Like thieves, they foster helplessness and violence. They galvanise new human perceptions and new mysteries of human relations.

In England, for example, a fresh spirit of egalitarianism emerges during the reign of the absolutist monarch Charles I. This culminates, following Charles' beheading and the civil war, in the Glorious Revolution of 1688, with its approbation of novel democratic principles, which themselves spread. Across the planet, over the next several centuries, new populations, often conceived in conditions of desperate malignancy, expand and linger. Warfare expands, until it embraces an infinite-seeming patriotic, racial and ideological butchery, and the menace of atomic apocalypse. The industrial revolution, chased by the electronic revolution of the late twentieth century, distributes and redistributes billions of people from farms into the modern city. The modern city, a planetary phenomenon by the last decade of the twentieth century, is itself the result of rapid public transportation, municipal police forces, as opposed to private ones or gangs, chatty wires, informative radio waves, artificial lighting, the invention of the flush toilet (by Sir John Harrington, who died in 1612) and refrigeration. The skyscrapers of New York and Hong Kong are the legacy of efficient sanitation and the universal availability of ice during sweaty summers.

One of the first casualties of the new attitude toward desire is the aesthetic experience, delicious to audiences of the Renaissance, of tragedy. What this means is the elimination of the guilt-sensitive hero who is sceptical about the divine or the cosmos. As an expanding concept of desire displaces beliefs in human limitations, tragedy comes to be viewed as an oddity. Eventually, it seems implausible. It must be explained. New ideas of tragedy must be invented. They too must soon be replaced. Any new idea of limitations must yield to subsequent convictions that any limitations at all are false, which becomes the theme of Baudelaire's nineteenth-century poem. Whenever limitations are discovered, hastily concocted new fantasies must replace the old accuracies of description. The result is a constantly ageing emotional terminology, and superb, scary confusion. Brooding is taken for melancholy, distraction for thoughtfulness, gloom for profundity, pathos for natural disorder, criminality for evil, evil for mere criminality and bathos for despair.

After three hundred years, a 'suspension of disbelief' is necessary to understand Lear's battle with his reptilian, snarling storm, and with the tempest in his head that means the doom of desire, or his mad, infinite notion of it, if not of the universe itself (a modern 'explanation' of the play). Beliefs in the rational and happy restraint of human emotions now indeed receive a regular bashing and pummelling. They are undermined by what the critic John Middleton Murry termed 'the *delectation* of the soul in the insufficiency and finally the annihilation of its own rationality'. Reason, conceived as a superfluous block to the impertinent strengths of the human mind, is itself popularly rejected.

None of this little sketch of the history of infinite desire is meant to suggest an unruffled development. In fact the new fashion smoulders in fits and starts. It even begins much earlier, and outside and ahead of science and the new astronomy. Its proper onset is to be found as early as the fourteenth and fifteenth centuries, and in at least two inventions that quite literally revolutionize how people see the world. The first is the invention of spectacles in Florence, probably by Salvino d'Armato (d. 1317). D'Armato's tomb, curiously enough, is located in the Church of Santa Maria Maggiore, where over a century later the painter Uccello (1396/7-1475) was to astonish people with the second invention. This appears in his painting of the Annunciation, which is the first work of pictorial art to present the idea of the vanishing point (*punto di fuga*).

Uccello's invention of a method whereby one could depict a three-dimensional scene in correct perspective on a two-dimensional plane surface, doing so with empirical accuracy, is arguably the more influential of these acts of imaginative shrewdness, but both show an intense new interest in optics, in how vision works and in how it may be extended and improved. They also, and the coincidence is revealing of the revolutionary nature of the experimentation of their age, solve the same optical problem, albeit in different ways, that of representing depth of vision to the mind.

Uccello's invention is almost immediately refined and perfected by Brunelleschi (1377-1446). It thereupon becomes the fulcrum of a complete shift in how painting is done. From the viewpoint of the history of infinite desire as well, however, and ultimately of modern guilt, the importance of Uccello's invention can scarcely be exaggerated. Painters of the ancient Greek and Roman world had mastered many of the problems of perspective, though there is no evidence that they understood either the concept of the vanishing point or the ratios of convergent lines needed to reproduce depth. Various *trompe l'oeil* murals from Pompeii and Boscoreale show a grasp of the geometry of vision and focus, if only across short, crowded spaces. Medieval artists, by contrast, busied themselves with heights and depths, with those of heaven and hell, rather than with level, earthbound expanses. Their enthusiasm bent itself upward and vertically, toward God and the Empyrean. They mistrusted the world shown to them by their eyes alone, regarding it – and optics – as a falsity. Hence their deliberate indifference to perspective, and the well-known semi-flatness of Romanesque and Gothic art.

Uccello, Brunelleschi and their successors opened a dramatic and power-producing vista onto the physical world, and onto perception itself. Their invention immediately acted as a hook, pulling painting more and more away from depictions of abstract spirituality into naturalistic experiences. This issue is also rather a subtler one than it at first appears to be. Uccello and his contemporaries certainly understood, despite their use of the term 'vanishing point', that what lay past the point had not actually vanished. It was merely invisible to the naked eye. Thus the unseen space beyond the vanishing point was to be hinted at in a special way: not as terminated or ended, but as infinite. If the invisible space beyond could not be grasped visually, it could still be sensed and imagined. It could even be admired and worshipped. In any case, it at once attracted and held the eye. It organized the picture at hand. This was inevitably the case because if the viewer's mind refused to surrender its focus to the new point, the very illusion of perspective, together with the illusion of vanishing vision, and the thrill of this new and special instance of imaginary blindness, collapsed entirely and the point remained a point. The trick lay in the geometry, which also corresponded to the meshed angles of sight of the newly invented spectacles – and to the natural behaviour of the eyes themselves.

As a relevant aside to this development, it should be noted that twentieth-century abstract art is chiefly distinguishable from the art of the Renaissance and later periods, including a good deal of Impressionist painting, not so much by its adventurous cubes, coils, parabolas and colours as by its blotting out, its complete elimination, of the vanishing point. In offering no equivalent centre for the viewer's intellectual and spiritual focus, and certainly none of the spiritual guidance that occurs in Romanesque and Gothic art either, it replaces Uccello's optical discovery with a purely subjective, though often stimulating, materialism: the properties of the painting itself, its paint, its colours, its subjective design, its brush strokes and, with abstract expressionist art, its cartwheeling dribbles. Its new infinity is that of illimitable shapes and states of mind that remain unguided by light, shadows and optics: its frequent presentation of a by now wholly internalized world of infinite desire.

A complete sketch of the history of optics would be extraneous to our purpose, which is to indicate the source of modern guilt in the brilliance and perversity of human reactions to the discovery of infinity. A few more broad strokes are essential, though. It was, for instance, a quest similar to Uccello's – to describe and explore actual deepness in space with greater accuracy – that prompted Galileo to train his weak telescope on the heavens, thus revealing their billowing immensities, along with the satellites of Jupiter and the lustrous rings of Saturn.

Galileo's telescope, which was no longer than a cigar, had been invented in Holland, and until he thought of it as an instrument for extending human knowledge of what is now called outer space, it was indulged as an amusing toy. On the other hand, the Pisan physicist shows his true motives most blatantly through his fascination not with astronomical depths but with infernal ones. In 1588, he gave two lectures before the Florentine Academy, in which, citing Archimedes' work in solid geometry as his basis of calculation, he offered estimates of the thickness of the sub-oceanic roof of Dante's Hell. He regarded these to us peculiar efforts as in no way unscientific. Indeed, as he and his contemporaries understood the matter, the geography of Hell below the ocean floor was as legitimate a field of scientific investigation as the extent of starry space.

Most early wranglings over the nature of light, and darkness too, were invariably cloaked in devout spiritual inquiries of this type. The empirical was simply another manifestation of the divine. Descartes and Newton, who placed the study of light on a modern scientific footing in the sixteenth century, were inflamed as much by a desire to understand God as to describe nature.

It was at this time that a valuable modern advance was made in predicting the behaviour of light according to strict mathematical laws. René Descartes (1596-1660), following Willibrord Snell (1591-1626), though he snootily refused to acknowledge Snell's prior work, discovered the law of light's bending or diffraction (it had first been discovered by the ancient Greeks). This was a law that took human understanding of natural phenomena very far from the assumptions of medieval thinkers that beams of light always moved in straight lines, and that these consisted of the straight lines of divine Reason. The law of diffraction predicted the precise angle of bending as light passed from one medium, such as air, into another, such as water. The next step, Newton's empirical definition of light itself, published in his *Opticks* (1704), was remarkable both for its lean clarity and its contemptuous indifference to superfluous metaphysical terms: 'By light therefore I understand, any being or power of a being (whether a substance of any power, action or quality of it) which proceeding directly from a lucid body, is apt to excite vision.' Light, it now appeared, could be described not in terms of some postulated 'meaning', or teleology, but solely according to its effect on the optic nerve.

Without intending to do so, Newton thus reinforced a view of infinity as purely materialistic, and possibly as without divine import. This view had in any case been growing along quite different lines among people curious about nature, including many of the better-read clergy, for some time. Doubts about the immortality of the soul had been rife since the late fifteenth century. Perceived correctly as a lethal threat to Church doc-

trine, they erupted into furious debates over whether there could
be life after death. The frenzied disagreements over this problem
culminated in the Lateran Council of 1513, which forbade the
teaching of any such notion, a philosophical stance in its own
right, and one modelled on the teachings of the Arab philosopher
Averroes (1126-98), who argued that the soul was mortal. Jacob
Burckhardt (1818-97) was among the first of the modern historians to discern in these religious and secular conflicts, as well as
in clerical corruption, the seeds of the Reformation. It must
nonetheless be acknowledged that the penalties for advocating
the idea of infinity remained severe well after it had commenced.
As late as 1600, the diplomat and mathematician Giordano
Bruno was burned at the stake for supporting Copernicus and
proclaiming that infinity must be a reality.

Each of these developments, or jousts with attitudes, bursts of
artistic and scientific insight, courageous acts of defiance and
spasms of grief over the imminent death of the old soul-suffused
universe – the marvellous and glittering house of planets and
God in which millions had found solace – indicates the turmoil
involved over centuries to demolish the architecture of past
beliefs and to set the new concepts of infinity and infinite desire
in their place. Frequently, as in the satires of Cervantes, Swift
and (in the twentieth century) Shaw and Orwell, the growing
imperialism of infinite desire is mocked, chastized for its lack of
ethics and hissed off the stage altogether. Nonetheless, its pro-
lific plants continue to sprout and its enormous tropical ferns and
palms, as well as its presumptuous northern evergreens, to
flourish, at first in dim and then in brighter glades, until they
reach at last into the valleys and even town lanes and city streets
of the entire world.

By 1805, William Wordsworth could count on popular comprehension and agreement when he wrote in *The Prelude* about the
terrors of desire baffled in its quest for a purer, better society,
and when he claimed that what happens in the human mind is
worse than any fantasies of chaos and hell:

    Not Chaos, not
The darkest pit of lowest Erebus,

Nor aught of blinder vacancy, scooped out
By help of dreams – can breed such fear and awe
As fall upon us often when we look
Into our Minds, into the Mind of Man –
My haunt, and the main region of my song.

Such sentiments, no matter how magnificent their expression, would have led to the madhouse a mere two centuries before. They were already beginning to provoke horrified suspicions that another, newer sort of madness might be developing in modern societies. Giacomo Leopardi (1798-1837) in his *Fragment on Suicide* connects Wordsworth's 'fear and awe', a dread emptiness, with knowledge and with surprisingly suicidal reactions to it:

What do all these voluntary [modern] deaths mean if not that men are tired and fiercely despairing of this existence? In ancient times men killed themselves as a heroic gesture, or for grand illusions, or from violent passions etc. etc. and their deaths were illustrious etc. But now that heroism and grand visions have disappeared, and passions are so sapped of energy, why is it that the number of suicides is so much greater? And not just among the great men who have failed in the grand manner, nourished on grand dreams, but men of all classes, so that even grand suicides are no longer 'illustrious'. ... It means that our knowledge of things brings about this desire for death. ... Men now take their lives coldly. (W.S. Di Piero trans.)

Passions, Leopardi argues, may be sapped, but desire – and some distinction between passion and desire remains crucial to him – is not. Where passion remains earthbound, the new forms of imaginative desire possess no restraints at all. It is desire that feasts on knowledge, or invented knowledge, or both. It is the condition of self-exhausting desire that begets the coldly undertaken suicides that Leopardi sees around him.

This condition, which seeks an always-denied response from the universe, from its apparent emptiness, Leopardi comes to describe with the curious word *noia*. The term as he uses it refers to a singular emotional and philosophical condition, beyond *ennui* and *accidie*, the sin described by Chaucer as torpor or sloth. It is the *noncuranza*, or indifference, that begins with his arrival as a young man in Rome from Recanti, and his nightmare vision of Rome as a city of monstrous infinity and tedium:

> In a big [modern] city a man lives without any relation whatsoever to the things around him; the context is so vast that no individual can possibly fill it or even be fully *aware* of it ... You can imagine, then, how much greater – and how much more terrible – the tedium of a great city must be than that of a small town. Human indifference, which is a horrible feeling, or rather an *absence* of feeling, must inevitably be concentrated in big cities. (Letter to his brother Carlo, 1825; W.S. Di Piero trans.)

Quite early, therefore, Leopardi is conscious of expanding the meaning of *noia* beyond its medieval senses of pain and interminable suffering. In his *Zibaldone* (entry for 30 September 1821), he speaks of it as 'the most sterile of human passions. It is the child of nullity and thus the mother of nothingness.' It is 'an emptiness of the soul', and as W.S. Di Piero observes, 'inseparable from yearning and desire and the failure of huge imaginative passions'. In extreme forms, *noia* rejects both civilization and nature. It comes to resemble the all-pervasive, reason-rejecting and tortured *ennui* of Des Esseintes, for instance, in Huysmans' *À rebours* (1884), or the predatory, irrational and feverish *ennui* of Flaubert's Emma Bovary.

Huysmans' Des Esseintes, exhausted with the emotional demands of human companionship, wishes to retreat into an infinity of beautiful objects, in which his desire for an aesthetically perfect and now lost universe will forever be sated, with splendid artifacts replacing the ugly, petty and new universe and its obsolescent spirituality. Emma Bovary, in search of an invented paradise of passion, one that will similarly supplant the mortal, new universe of mundane pleasures and sorrows, seeks an ecstasy surpassing the relief of the suicide, and triumphant over the heaven of morally irrelevant saints.

Noia, as Leopardi describes it, often also induces a macabre, dark enthusiasm. The man or woman experiencing this stimulating condition may strangely rejoice, not in the discovery that the universe is inadequate, but in bringing the news of its inadequacy back to others. Such a person will seem to return in lonely delight from a slaughter on a frightful frontier, or sounding like the fateful messenger in the Book of Job, although for Job the world is alive with divine justice: 'And I only am escaped alone to tell thee.' This new beshrouded ecstasy is the deeper emotion of Baudelaire's already cited 'Le Voyage', with its modernistic report on infinite and totemic desire as leading into a fatuous pursuit of novelty for its own sake, and eventually into the thuggery of death:

Ô Mort, vieux capitaine, il est temps! levons l'ancre.
Ce pays nous ennuie, Ô Mort! Appareillons!
Si le ciel et la mer sont noirs comme de l'encre,
Nos coeurs que tu connais sont remplis de rayons!

Verse-nous ton poison pour qu'il nous réconforte!
Nous voulons, tant ce feu nous brûle le cerveau,
Plonger au fond du gouffre, Enfer ou Ciel, qu'importe?
Au fond de l'Inconnu pour trouver de *nouveau*!

[O death, old captain, it's time to hoist the anchor!
This country bores us, death – let's go our ways!
Though sky and sea are inky, turning blacker,
You know our hearts are full of shining rays!

Give us your poison! Its fire slakes our fear!
We'll plumb (as its fire burns our brains right through)
The deep Abyss – Hell, Heaven, we don't care –
For Depths Unknown, to hunt out what is *new*!]

Everything, suddenly, is to be sacrificed to what is 'nouveau', which will be welcome whether it be hellish or heavenly. What the 'nouveau' must clearly not be, however, is ordinary experience, experience of 'ce pays', or of anything finite. Even the poison of death, an acrid accomplice on this quest, is welcome – let it pour into us, granting us ease – precisely because it burns away our brains, or reason, the venerable and finite universe of divine intelligence.

These are not merely the sentiments of Romanticism, or of its successor, Existentialism, nor is *noia* in any sense to be seen as a phenomenon whose fashion is limited to the Romantic and Existentialist periods. In fact 'Romanticism' itself, as a term conjuring up a special sort of literature, painting, music and way of life, is meaningless unless placed in its proper context of the history of desire. There the Romantic recipe of nostalgia, of imagination as a *nouvelle* religion, of mysticism, of rebellion and of an obsessively voluptuous apprehension of reality, makes perfect sense. Romanticism is an expected result of the desertion of finitude. Shelley's meditation in the Protestant cemetery at Rome is but one logical consequence of infinity and idolized forms of desire. So too is Keats' remark, characteristic of any poet or reporter stricken with *noia*, in a letter to his brother George (November 1818), that 'the more we know the more inadequacy we discover in the world to satisfy us'.

2. The Unappeasable God

In the modern Western world, infinite personal desire has replaced God. It possesses many of the same powers as the old and now mostly dead god of Christians, Jews and others – of omnipotence and omniscience, for instance, though it is not quite so good at miracles – plus a vastly and paradoxically greater capacity to inspire guilt. It is infinitely subtle, and has no trouble in assuming a Christian or Jewish or Islamic disguise for the sake of many of its believers, who for social and psychological reasons wish to continue calling themselves Christians, Jews, Moslems and other things. Its adaptability, its complete elasticity, is one of its most commendable and bewildering qualities.

Nonetheless, one cannot escape the conclusion that this widely worshipped and also despised god is merely the divine incarnation of solipsism. For millions, the individual human mind, with its ever-ballooning wishes, has replaced the universe. Jean Jacques Rousseau (1712-78) declared that God exists because he said so. This type of subjective substitute for facts, texts, rituals and investigations, which operates by arrogating a priestly role to mere impressions and emotions, has by now become a popular method of avoiding hard questions of truth about the real universe. Rousseau has managed an immense, terrifying victory. Eden too, and for some hell, have been skilfully reinvigorated in restricted mental landscapes. As Felicia D. Hemans (1793-1835) notes in 'The Abencerrage' (Canto I), however, 'There smiles no Paradise on earth so fair/ But guilt will raise avenging phantoms there.' All is not as easy as it looks.

At the close of the nineteenth century, Nietzsche's Zarathustra had already announced that 'God is dead' (actually he was not the first to do so, and Dostoyevski's Matryosha likewise entertains the grim fancy that she has killed God). Whether or not Nietzsche's statement is meant as a criticism of an irrelevant and dying religion, or as a revelation to which he had gained special access, it can scarcely mitigate the guilt automatically issuing from the new god of infinite desire. The reason lies in this god's cruel new espionage practised on the soul, and in the desperate yet acquiescent condition of its adherents.

Paradoxically, most of these adherents must feel much freer than their traditionally religious or non-religious predecessors, and especially from superstition. Their opportunities must seem flatteringly abundant. Their actual condition, however, cannot be different from what Gibbon observes in describing the political manipulations of Augustus: 'Augustus was sensible that mankind is governed by names; nor was he deceived in his expectation that the senate and people would submit to slavery, provided they were respectfully assured that they still enjoyed their ancient freedom' (*The Decline and Fall of the Roman Empire*, I; 1776).

In fact for many modern people, the golden calf, Baal, Isis, Zeus, Dis and Odin, together with the ancient Greek muses of inspiration, have simply rematerialized, and are strangely accompanied by resurrections of the old versions of the God of

Christians, Jews and Moslems. They form in the modern brain a
vast, puffy, apparently pleasant god-soufflé. This pantheon of the
world's lost divinities is available in private to any modern soul
surrendered to the ultimate god of infinite desire, and the soufflé,
which is also infinitely tasty because baked according to individual preferences, quickly expands in the mind to fill it completely,
and bellies into the universe beyond it, spilling among its planets
and stars and pulsating nebulae, and floating past them, before
suddenly collapsing on itself in a paroxysm of unavoidable guilt.
The now-shrunk squib of guilt, like a mere dank nub at the centre
of the servile soul, goes on with a life of its own, and refuses to
rise or stir. One may chop at it. The chopped-off portion will
instantly be replaced. One may ignore it. It will gleam darkly,
commanding attention. One may rant, rave and seek distrac-
tions. The nub-like substance will simply endure. It may seem to
brood. It will probably grow heavier. Then, without warning, it
will lighten, blush with a horrible vampiristic blood-energy, rein-
flate, rise again, and the whole fantastic, shabby process will
repeat itself.

     This dreadful picture may clarify the fact that it is obviously
impossible to appease the new stupendous desire-god. Nothing
avails – not Buddhism, for instance, which seeks the death of
desire, but which cannot mean much to those many whose deity
can feign even self-elimination; and not most types of psychiatry,
which confuse sickness of the mind with sickness of the squan-
dered soul. As a result, one's reactions to the frustration
attending one's new predicament may be extreme. One may
regard oneself, in the manner of Kafka's Georg, as a helpless
failure. One may feel horribly maladjusted. One may feel diseased (a term which to medieval astrologers and physicians
actually meant that one was out of ease with the universe).
Society, culture and the state may seem alien. Their disconnect-
edness, or one's own, will have nothing to do with wealth, with
money. No amount of money or economic security, or bankruptcy,
will affect one's irremediable, unending guilt. Religion will seem
fraudulent. At best, it may briefly assuage fears of isolation, then
pull to pieces as one feels uncomfortable with its familiar, unso-

phisticated attempts to deal with the modern dilemma of facing and submitting to the demands of the desire-god.

Sex, love and marriage may also only mark various limits of one's vain efforts to satisfy it. It cannot be satisfied. No materialistic god can be mollified. No sacrifice can alter its chill cyncism. Often sex, love and marriage may themselves succumb to its divine implacability. Nor can one be assisted by changing one's address. If one retreats into the countryside, one may feel guilt over abandoning the city. If one remains in a city, the god will seem to track one down at one's apartment or house, or simply brush about one in the streets. The sterile flatness of one's existence at this point, a secret concealed from others and often from oneself, amid crowds that blandish warm, empty smiles and meaningless promises, will perhaps only restimulate one's vast guilty sense of inadequacy. For millions, this feeling has become their latest acknowledgement of the guilt that cannot, it seems, be escaped. If this guilt is in some sense the result of Renaissance and later art and science, it has thus exceeded and perverted their wildest and most depressing ambitions. The burlesqued idols of the ancient world have been granted a dour second chance, and a great expansion of their strengths, turning, together with infinite numbers of private whims, into an ever-demanding, always intimidating god-abstraction that dominates many thoughts.

This is why as well, in modern times, the sweet opposite of guilt seems scarcely to exist, and why, even when it does, it can only seldom take the form of joyous innocence. Millions of seemingly innocent people feel guilty. They have committed no crimes, nor are the wrongs that they may have inflicted on others more than they need be ashamed of, and that in the vast majority of cases they might easily make amends for. Nonetheless their guilt persists, at least in their own eyes, and often folded tidily away, though it cannot help but inject their other emotions and acts with unmentioned pain. Sometimes they succeed in reassigning their guilt to people who are likewise apparently innocent, because it is too torturous to be borne alone. It may then make a hideous mockery, a spiteful jape, of perfectly decent relationships, ruining them or shuttling them into agonizing perverse gardens where fresh tortures cause their destruction.

Prior to the twentieth century in the West, as we have seen, people often assumed that the guilt of the seemingly innocent arose from the inferior position of all human beings in relation to God, and that broken pacts with God must be the source of most feelings of guilty worthlessness. This was a happier situation, because it implied atonement. In the presence of the new god of infinite desire, however, the idea of atonement has lost its meaning. With the loss of finitude has come the loss of acceptable forgiveness.

All this is on the negative side, but before coming to the positive, we must take more unpleasant facts into account. It is interesting that adults who seem guilt-free may be diagnosed by psychologists as sociopaths. Usually it is the criminal, and especially the homicidal maniac, that they have in mind, but the point is that the psychologist tends to regard the guilt-liberated person as mentally ill. Complete freedom from guilt is viewed as a debilitation (much as the Church, or traditional rabbinical Judaism, might still see it). A well-honed guilt sense, or at least a sense of guilty empathy, is considered normal and a promoter of social peace. To be sure, guilt may act as a useful leash on some potential murderers, rapists and thieves, but it should be clear that other restraints are just as effective. One is the police, whose deterrent presence may mean fear of capture rather than guilt. Another is the simple knowledge that crime is wrong. Whether it is wrong in some universal or natural sense makes no difference. Large numbers of people surely refrain from violent assaults not because they might feel guilty afterwards, but because the idea of such behaviour is repellent to them, far more so than the acts of injustice that they have experienced. A very great many, possibly a majority, discipline themselves because at bottom their love of human beings makes it impossible for them to accept vengeance as a way of life. It is impractical to deride the power of love, though this is often done, and to slight its immense efficiency in improving millions of ordinary lives.

It is also unrealistic to apply Western criteria of automatic guilt willy-nilly to everyone. Religions such as Hinduism and

Mohammedanism, as previously noted, subscribe to few or none of these concepts. Neither do certain other religions. Traditional Japanese Shintoism, for example, involves implicit pacts with one's ancestors, according to which one will respect and even worship them, but no notion of primal or intrinsic guilt. Shintoist ethics, moreover, are determined solely by community values. They entail shame, and even what may be termed profound shame, or loss of face, which in extreme circumstances may lead to the suicide of the offender, but given the purely social issues involved, no guilt of the cosmos-insulting type. The Japanese concept of *giri*, according to which one owes another a debt or obligation, is not guilt in this sense; neither is the Old English and pre-Christian *gylt*, from which the modern English word is derived, and which likewise refers to indebtedness to another. Chinese folk religion, before the Han period (206 BC), lacked notions of sin and guilt. Offences committed against various deities were regarded as essentially identical to those committed against neighbours and enemies, though because the gods were more powerful, divine punishment could conceivably be more austere. The islanders of Polynesia (including Fiji, Tokelau and Samoa) are uninterested in guilt, apart from criminal guilt, and sin, and oblivious to the idea of primal guilt.

All this suggests that recent scientific investigations into whether there may be a genetic predisposition to human guilt are too drastically conceived along mechanistic lines, which is not the same as saying that they are useless. Galen Strawson ('In deepest sympathy', *Times Literary Supplement*, 29 November 1996) observes that a genetic proneness to altruism, revenge, regret, shame and guilt, if it exists, is no doubt itself deeply influenced by adaptive psychological manoeuvres, cultural factors and ultimately by individual choices. This requires deeper examination.

Any purely materialistic or mechanistic argument for human guilt, as for other forms of human behaviour – to wit, that we succumb to guilty feelings even when we are not guilty because we are 'programmed' to do so – should probably be rejected on purely philosophical grounds. The chief objections to it are that it fails to account for all the facts about human beings and the universe, and that it requires as much of a leap of faith as a belief in God, but in a different, colder direction. To these there must be added a secondary objection: that it often appeals to the arrogance of those who seek to deny all mystery to the universe, and to its origins, as if these had been cleared up by mechanical and physical explanations, or soon would be, when nothing of the sort has been done or could be done.

Indeed, a significant problem with the materialist outlook is the same as that with religion and theology: an absence of any sensible account of the reason for everything. Materialists, and some scientists, often seek to opt out of this question by denying its relevance or by saying that it is not what they deal with, but this cannot be accepted. If an ultimate claim is made, a satisfactory and complete answer must be supplied. Otherwise the claim is merely false or unproved, and the argument must be regarded as no more persuasive than Rousseau's solipsistic, subjective 'proof' of the existence of God.

Beyond these swamps of motives, mystery and incompleteness, the materialist position also reduces all matters of human free will and ethics, and guilt is above all a matter of ethics, to groups of deterministic social forces and electrical impulses, plus a few proteins. The reduction of choice to mechanics is actually an ancient Greek idea, though only Democritus (460-361 BC) is known to have espoused it with influential and misanthropic enthusiasm (some materialists, such as Epicurus (341-270 BC) were not complete determinists, allowing for brief spasms of a weak type of free will, but only at the atomic level).

There are at least two objections to this proposition as well, one practical, the other not so practical but more substantial and important. To deal with the practical objection first: it involves the acceptance of a thoroughly gloomy comprehension of human existence, by maintaining that people are completely without responsibility for their acts. They are simply machines, or machine-like, and creak, scramble, race and leap along egotistically. Altruism, self-sacrifice and ethics are seen as mere camouflaging tarpaulins tossed over mechanical defences and material requirements.

It is obvious, however, that on this puppeteering basis, no society except one rooted in authoritarian and totalitarian lashings would continue to function at all. There would be no more sense in restoring a sick person to health with appropriate medical treatment, for instance, than in repairing a malfunctioning car – in fact less, since the car at least has an agreed use and can often be repaired, while the sick and the old, and especially anyone who disagrees with those in charge and their materialist outlook, and who might conceivably cause rebellion among the rest, could far more profitably be eliminated. Ghastly policies to this effect have indeed been carried out by ancient and modern authoritarian societies. The basis of these policies, and the heart of all philosophical problems with materialism itself, is in fact its presupposition that, as with any machine, future human behaviour can be predicted on the basis of past behaviour. Little in history can be cited to support this crude notion, while there is a great deal that must discredit it, such as (to cite two examples only) the failure of the Marxist theory of history to make accurate predictions (hence necessitating its constant revisions), and the astonishing and courageous acts of disobedience by some citizens of authoritarian societies, and also by people subsisting in authoritarian families, who have been conditioned by punishments to keep a slavish silence.

The second objection is that the materialist wishes much less to describe human beings than to redefine them to suit his assumptions. His outlook is deductive, and as such is reminiscent of the cart-before-the-horse method of medieval theologians. Materialism, in other words, is willing to admit the reality of only two dimensions of human existence: the physical and the emotional-intellectual (though the assumption here is that the second of these will eventually be shown to be physical as well). This line of thought deliberately disregards the possibility of the existence of a spiritual dimension. Spirituality in the materialist's view is a mere delusion. There can, however, be no compelling reason for believing this either, except that the materialist wishes to believe it, and has adopted the irrational premise that as the spiritual is not physical, and as he or she has not experienced it, it cannot exist.

Overwhelming evidence contradicts any such possibility. This evidence, moreover, has nothing to do with the actual contents of

the spiritual dimension – with specific religious beliefs, for example, or with forms of mysticism, superstitions and even
convictions about divinely inspired guilt – any more than accepting the reality of the physical dimension requires accepting the
existence of specific types of physical phenomena. The evidence
for a spiritual dimension is at least twofold: the universality and
antiquity of spiritual passions, on the one hand, and, on the
other, the apparent impossibility of destroying them. The first of
these is self-evident, but the second must be considered briefly,
because it indicates other dangers in materialistic doctrines
themselves.

During the twentieth century alone, the fiercest assaults have
been launched on religion, particularly by communist, Fascist
and Nazi régimes, in an attempt to replace it with materialism.
The failure of these activities, which have led to unspeakable
violence, along with genocide, and the collapse and disappear-
ance of the régimes themselves, must argue the invincible
tenacity of human spirituality. It must also support a quite
frightening conclusion, that materialism of whatever stripe rapidly becomes unfeeling in private and totalitarian in public.
Though advocated by some who may not realize its implications,
this outlook, especially in the political arena, cannot in the end
be understood as much more than an ill-contrived excuse for
usurping absolute power over others. In view of both these likely
facts, it may not be far-fetched to imagine that the materialist
has actually chosen to ignore the spiritual attic in the mind, or
as Plato urges, in the mansion of the soul, leaving it empty, while
pretending that it has been demolished. A famished madwoman
or madman may haunt about it, however, awaiting a compassionate reprieve.

This is not the place to enter into a final difficulty with
materialism, whether the mind, or self, as opposed to the merely
mechanical brain, can be proved to exist as well. Roger Penrose
(in *The Emperor's New Mind* and other books) has advanced
strong arguments to demonstrate that it indeed exists, but the
complete rejection of the materialist-mechanist position proposed here may reinforce an all-but-obvious truth: that hard and
adventurous choices, taken by human beings together and in

isolation throughout history, have led humanity into its present opportunity and predicament.

It is a predicament, first, that repeatedly announces its presence in everyday life. With the god of infinite desire as the god of infinite guilt, and with the old methods of atonement and confession rendered superfluous for many, the ancient safety valves have been blocked, the guilt-chambers capped. With nowhere to go, the new guilt steams and presses, leaking out where it can. False ideas of it become commonplace. Often it slips into conversation as a substitute for embarrassment, remorse, shame, regret and responsibility. This misuse of the term is probably no accident, or the result of a desire to sound impressive ('I feel guilty about getting to the office late'; 'I feel guilty about forgetting the candles', or the wine, or the dry cleaning). Nor is the misuse a consequence of the word 'guilt' being shorter or more convenient. There are other ways to say these things, and people often find them. The kickback of 'guilt' into minor encounters, in which it is falsely used, often seems to suggest a morbid aspect of the modern guilt-phenomenon itself: that its energy can indeed find no easy release, and that it therefore pops up in spots where it must at first seem a mere theatrical device.

Despite the rampage of modern guilt through modern societies, however, it remains as absurd to speak of the universe as permeated with guilt as to speak of it as permeated with bad weather. Guilt and weather are human concepts, and earthly ones, even if they are also acts of God. The idea of a galactic wind, or of an intra-galactic storm of asteroids, is just a metaphor, and one so banal that no poet worth his salt would dream of using it. Suffice it that galactic winds and storms of asteroids do not exist, that these are purely anthropomorphic notions, and that the idea of some universal guilt spreading beyond the moon is also only a metaphor. It appears a flimsy one too, if we consider that there are probably intelligent creatures on other worlds who have their own, no doubt drastically different, problems.

The fact is – and this seems to be our genuine predicament – that the human species is experiencing, as always, a period of dramatic adjustment to its new knowledge about its environment. Much of this knowledge is several hundred years old by now – that concerning infinity, for instance – but this matters little in terms of the fundamental changes in outlook that are needed and that are developing. Early reactions to any perceived psychological threat are likely to be extreme. Afterwards, a settling down into a new balance may be anticipated. Even extreme reactions have their values. Thus the violence with which the Church greeted the new astronomy, and the new fashion of infinite desire, has acted as a spur to art, science and the spread of democracy. In the foreseeable future, it is reasonable to await new thrashings about of spiritual beliefs, and of organized religion, as people strive to release themselves from the shadowy threats of modern guilt, or at least to find fresh and sane ways to deal with it.

In the meantime, a delicious innocence – an opportunity – as always in the past, surrounds us on all sides. This is not the old innocence of purity. Its colours are not the foams and ambers of the biblical milk and honey, nor its notes those of angelic hosannahs. Its more mundane perfumes, textures and tastes are more familiar and no less appeasing of the modern guilt-pain. We partake of them often, though with a sense of loss for the more fanatical and the more guilt-entangled among us, whose release is not so easy, or which may never come about.

For instance, we recognize that it would be impossible for us to run over to the apartment in which Kafka's Georg lives with his ferocious father, and tell him, before he rushes out to drown himself, to take time to stop and consider the changed cosmos and the history of guilt, remarking that if he were to do so, he might see the miserable irrelevance of what he is about to do, that his guilty pain might be alleviated by cosmic readjustment. By the time we meet him, Georg's anguish has become too unbearable for any such dream of rescue to make sense. We also see that we could never simply grasp Dostoyevski's Stavrogin by the lapels, shake him a bit and announce that his guilty criminal ambitions are probably one unintended result of the invention of spectacles in the fourteenth century. He would think that he knew better.

We realize that we would never be able to transmit to either of them the miraculous nectar, the secret of the freedom that is in fact available and that rinses and cleanses our souls. This secret is quite simply that no one can sustain a perfect loyalty to any god at all, even the god of infinite modern guilt, year in year out, day after day. The heart rebels against the mind, the mind against the heart. The guilty among us must often enjoy instants and even moments, and more, of shining freedom. Perhaps one evening at a concert Wagner's overture to *The Flying Dutchman* is played. As we listen to it, we at once understand, and probably cannot help doing so, that even though the composer was guilty of the most appalling bigotry, and devoted much of his life to repugnant power-seeking, his music is free – utterly, resoundingly free. The horns and oboes set before us a fiery cathedral of sound, which belongs to no god at all, including the gods of music, though perhaps to another, more traditional God alone, if one still accepts the old notion, and vast experiences of love more blissful than Wagner himself may have understood.

Or we may decide to read, and read again, Guy de Maupassant's little story, 'Madame Tellier's Establishment', an enamelled companion piece to his 'Two Friends', but one without its prophetic innuendos of casual guilty slaughter, slavery and treason. In this earlier story, Madame Tellier, who runs a whorehouse in a small town in Normandy, decides to take her entire staff of five prostitutes off to her twelve-year-old niece's First Communion. The story presents no real plot. There is scarcely any tension. There are also few conflicts – some petty rivalries which simply evaporate. The author dishes up an extraordinary holiday, and heaps of unrestrained life.

We climb aboard a train with the six gaily dressed women, then meet a garter salesman who teases them and gives them each a free sample. Later, we transfer with them to a horse-drawn cart, in which they are jostled ridiculously about on loose chairs as they are conducted through a warm countryside glowing with red poppies. Then comes their arrival at the village, plus their overnight stay and the communion ceremony itself, with cheerful villagers nicely turned out and proud of their children; then the lavish party afterwards – and then, presto, the women are back home and at work again (they enjoy their work, it seems, and their familiar clientele). There is a certain plush simplicity to each of these events, but no sense of struggle at all.

If this is the case, though, what holds us to the story? Whence our almost but not quite alienated fascination? It is only when one asks these questions that one becomes aware of Maupassant's genius trimming every phrase. The tension, one realizes, has been growing not in the story but in oneself as one reads. It has emerged from one's constant expectation, no doubt based on one's own life but toyed with in a friendly way by Maupassant, that something unpleasant must happen. A disturbance must arise. It never does. One expects, for instance, some crude judgement to be passed on these women – common, jolly creatures, as all the village can see, who have the nerve to descend on a holy ceremony. They are greeted with enthusiasm and misplaced congratulations on their devoutness. One anticipates some vulgar, neurotic outburst. This is never so much as hinted at. Above all, one guesses that Maupassant himself will smuggle a subtle imputation of guilt into their blithe merry-making. This, too, does not occur, and his style retains its crisp lightness. What one does get is a set of rural summer scenes in which everybody has a good time. That is all. It is entirely all, and of guilt of any type there is not a trace.

Select Bibliography

The books listed here supplement those mentioned in the text proper, and may serve as essential further reading.

Amato, J.A., *Guilt and Gratitude: A Study of the Origins of Contemporary Conscience* (Greenwood, Conn., 1982).

Eberhard, W., *Guilt and Shame in Traditional China* (Berkeley, 1967).

Evans, G.R., *Augustine on Evil* (Cambridge, Eng., 1982).

Fung, Yu-Lan, *A History of Chinese Philosophy*. 2 vols. Derk Bodde trans. (London, 1953).

Girard, R., *Violence and the Sacred* (Baltimore, 1979).

MacIntyre, A., *A Short History of Ethics: A History of Moral Philosophy from the Homeric Age to the Twentieth Century* (London, 1981).

Mayer, A.C., *Culture and Morality* (Oxford, 1981).

Morris, H., *Guilt and Shame* (Berkeley, 1971).

Nakane, C., *Japanese Society* (London, 1970).

Ohly, F., *The Damned and the Elect: Guilt in Western Culture*, Linda Archibald trans., Foreword by George Steiner (Cambridge, Eng., 1992).

Parkin, D., ed., *The Anthropology of Evil* (Oxford, 1985).

Piers, G., *Shame and Guilt: A Psychoanalytic and Cultural Study* (New York, 1971).

Reik, T., *Myth and Guilt* (New York, 1957).

Ricoeur, P., *The Symbolism of Evil* (Boston, 1967).

Spaemann, R., *Basic Moral Concepts* (London, 1989).

Weber, M., *The Religion of India*, trans. and ed. by H.H. Garth and D. Martindale (Glencoe, Ill., 1958).

Index